2/10

D0723364

The
Divorce Prevention
Handbook

The Divorce Prevention Handbook

✦

A Practical Guide for Saving Marriages

Richard Rein, Ph.D.

iUniverse, Inc.

New York Lincoln Shanghai

The Divorce Prevention Handbook
A Practical Guide for Saving Marriages

iUniverse books may be ordered through booksellers or by contacting:

iUniverse
2021 Pine Lake Road, Suite 100
Lincoln, NE 68512
www.iuniverse.com
1-800-Authors (1-800-288-4677)

The views expressed in this work are solely those of the author and do not necessarily reflect the views of the publisher, and the publisher hereby disclaims any responsibility for them.

ISBN-13: 978-0-595-38604-8 (pbk)
ISBN-13: 978-0-595-82985-9 (ebk)
ISBN-10: 0-595-38604-0 (pbk)
ISBN-10: 0-595-82985-6 (ebk)

Printed in the United States of America

For my wife Cathy, who teaches me about the joy of relationships.

Contents

1

Saving Marriages

I meet many families in the course of my work as a psychologist. In one such family, a woman I will call Kristin brought her daughter, Barbara, for help with Barbara's behavioral issues. We were able to work through Barbara's issues, and all seemed well.

But a few years later, Kristin called to see if I was again available to see Barbara. Kristin told me that she and her husband Frank had consulted their attorneys about pursuing a divorce. Kristin was concerned that Barbara's behavioral issues would return.

I am troubled when I hear about a child forced to deal with divorce. Single parents and their kids seem to struggle more than families with two involved parents. Before I agreed to help their daughter cope with divorce, I wanted to know if there was any hope for the marriage. I asked Kristin what was occurring between her husband and her.

Kristin: I recently discovered that my husband Frank was having an affair with a co-worker. I can't believe that he would do that to me. I'm just worried about how Barbara will deal with it.
Dr. Rein: I know you're worried about Barbara, but have you and Frank seen a marriage counselor at any point?
Kristin: No. I'm not sure that there's much hope for this marriage now.
Dr. Rein: Would you be willing to see a marriage counselor before making such a large decision?
Kristin: I'll consider it and talk to Frank.

Kristin's decision to divorce would end a twelve-year marriage. Barbara and her siblings would have to deal with the stress and potential emotional suffering of living in two households. Fortunately, after our conversation,

Kristin and Frank agreed to work on the underlying problems that caused Frank to stray from the marriage. By addressing these issues with me, they were able to discuss and resolve problems that they would never have been able to resolve on their own.

I have practiced as a licensed psychologist for over twenty years. During that time I have worked with thousands of patients and have discovered approaches that are quite effective for resolving significant marital conflict. This has allowed me to return hundreds of couples from the brink of divorce to happy, fulfilling relationships. In this book, I share my observations from my work with couples to help you resolve problems in your marriage. By employing the approaches outlined later, Kristin and Frank resolved their differences and avoided divorce. I never needed to help their daughter Barbara deal with the negative impact of divorce.

Marriages carry so many of our hopes for the future when they begin. Intimate relationships bring so much pleasure: dinners, movies, long walks, pleasant conversation reflecting on life, and the enjoyment of raising children together. However, some couples are miserable with each other. Their time together is full of conflict and pain. They reach a point in their relationship where they can no longer heal their differences. They move toward hatred or exist in a loveless marriage.

All of this conflict and pain is avoidable. If couples learn skills and techniques to help them interact more compassionately and respectfully with one another, they can add depth and richness to their lives. How many people enjoy going to a movie or a restaurant alone? Most of us prefer to share our experiences with another. We hope to be with someone we respect and care for and who cares for and respects us.

Couples can enhance their marriages by learning to talk with each other differently. Many couples have not had great role models for healthy, functioning relationships. They need to learn the skills of talking with each other in a way that enhances the relationship.

The goal of this book is to help couples reverse the potential deterioration of their relationships. Couples can learn when they are interacting in an unhealthy manner and gain the skills to communicate effectively with each other. Couples can regain hope and a shared future if they are willing to do some hard work.

In this book, the reader will find many successful and effective strategies for helping couples address difficult conflicts. Couples in distress can apply these principles to their marriages and improve their relationships. Sometimes readers may feel they need more help than a book can provide. They may need skilled professionals to intervene and change their communication patterns. This change can help them leave unhealthy dynamics rather than leaving each other.

THE GENERAL CONTRACTOR

The decision to seek professional help is a difficult step for many couples. Some see it as a defeat when they are unable to work out their problems on their own. Some couples have difficulty opening up to a stranger about something as intimate as their relationship.

The average couple doesn't seek marital therapy until seven years after they identify significant marital problems (Gottman and Silver 2000). Unfortunately, many relationships deteriorate beyond repair before the couple seeks professional help. This could explain why fifty percent of first marriages and sixty percent of remarriages end in divorce.

Couples are much more likely to repair conflicts and differences early in their relationship. However, eventually some couples in distress develop a communication style that does not allow them to repair relationship conflict. The relationship deteriorates over time. It is very difficult for a couple to change a dysfunctional communication pattern on their own. This is when a relationship needs professional help.

A person who is handy around the house might be able to repair leaky faucets and change light switches. However, if a house needs a major rehabilitation, most people would need to call in a general contractor. Unfortunately, sometimes the call to the contractor is easier to make than the call for repairs to a marriage.

Many couples like those that wait seven years to make the call for help never make the call at all. Seven years is a long time to be in a conflicted or distant relationship. What if there were a way to get the couple help before the point that their marriage dissolved? That is certainly the purpose of professional intervention.

The role of the professional is to teach an individual the skills to talk successfully with his or her spouse. Good communication skills are necessary to address day-to-day or underlying issues. Often people are unaware of their own contribution to the conflict or disconnection in their relationship. It is the job of the professional to analyze the interactions between the couple and point out which processes are preventing the couple from communicating well.

A professional gets to observe the couple's interactions. The professional will point out communication patterns and teach the couple how to relate differently. Eventually spouses will learn to identify their own unhealthy communication styles and change how they interact with one another without a professional being present.

If marital conflict is in its early stages, the couple may be able to resolve issues independently by applying some of the principles in this book. However, if doing so is not sufficient, please consider working with a professional. If previous counseling was unsuccessful, shop for a professional who can deliver more effective results. A marriage is too important to neglect, especially if children will be affected by a breakup.

ON THE FENCE

Many couples who enter treatment are unsure whether they will continue their marriage. One or both spouses are dissatisfied and want to change the status quo of the relationship. The underlying message is that if the relationship does not change, they are not going to remain together as a couple. If they choose to stay, they may endure a loveless marriage or a marriage of misery.

Some couples see professional intervention as the last resort before contacting their attorneys. Couples who start counseling earlier in their marriages want to see if they can improve the relationship. They are dissatisfied but not necessarily at the point of pursuing a divorce. However, they may be aware that if the relationship continues to deteriorate, divorce is a possibility.

Couples seeking professional help typically want to save their marriage. Although the couple is not initially sure if the relationship can be saved, they hope that the relationship will improve. They need to have successful experiences to prove that their relationship is worth saving. The professional provides these opportunities during their work together.

It is important that the professional does *not* allow the couple to repeat their unsuccessful exchanges in the meetings. The professional's job is to have couples talk about their relationship issues in a successful manner. If spouses can begin to have successful exchanges, this provides a glimmer of hope and can motivate a couple to change how they interact with one another.

Early in treatment, the purpose is to help partners understand their relationship dynamics. Couples in conflict are often not aware of their relationship dynamics and communication patterns. It is as if they are in a maze and don't know how to get out.

The professional with an expert perspective and a history of successfully guiding couples out of mazes is something a couple considering counseling specifically wants to look for. It is as if the professional is above the maze and can see how the couple gets stuck, tell them how it happens, and direct the couple how to reverse course and successfully maneuver through the maze.

It is very frustrating for a couple when they get stuck in the relationship maze. The individuals involved tend to lose perspective and criticize and blame one another for getting lost. The professional aids the couple in regaining perspective and learning the skills to maneuver successfully through the maze.

WHAT PROBLEMS?

Women are frequently the emotional barometers in the relationship. Women often sense before men when a lack of emotional connectedness will result in a problematic situation. In the same way that a barometer's drop in pressure can indicate an impending storm, women have the ability to measure the overall emotional connection in a relationship. If there is an emotional disconnection in the marriage, a wife will often sense it before her husband. It is important for men to be responsive to their wives' dissatisfaction. If they ignore it, wives may eventually become so emotionally distant, that the marriage may not be able to recover.

When women realize a disconnection has taken place, they may insist on counseling. Sometimes the wife threatens to end the marriage unless her husband joins her in seeking help for their relationship. The husband may acknowledge that there are issues but feel the problems are not to the extent that the couple needs professional intervention.

Women describe greater awareness of their own emotional lives and the need for greater emotional connection with their partners. If a woman's emotional needs are neglected in the marriage, conflict and emotional distance are the result.

Women have a tendency to address their issues by talking about them. When they talk, they can see their issues out in front of them and get the clear perspective they need to resolve their issues.

Men typically address their issues by withdrawing, figuring out their issues on their own, and maybe eventually sharing the results of their internal discovery. When women share their issues with them, men tend to try to fix the problem (Gray 1992). This typically annoys women; they are not looking for a solution to a problem but for a supportive and listening ear. Listening is a crucial skill for men to learn.

When a husband listens well, he is more likely to attend to a woman's emotional needs. The marriage may experience less disconnection as a result. Therefore it is important for husbands to be attentive to their wives' emotional worlds.

The quality of emotional sensitivity is not the exclusive domain of women. Since it is more typical of marriages, it is presented that way. However, there are certainly numerous relationships in which the husband is more emotionally sensitive than his wife. In these cases, the male-female dynamics are reversed.

YOU TREAT STRANGERS BETTER THAN ME

Mary and Steve are in their midtwenties and recently had a baby. Mary was a stay-at-home mom, and Steve was a supervisor in the construction field. Mary was starting to see someone else, which served as an alarm that she and Steve needed professional help.

Steve liked to get together with his co-workers after work. They would frequently stop at a neighborhood bar for drinks. Steve often came home late for dinner. If he called to say he was going to stay out later, he still rarely came home at the time he said he would. Mary grew weary of this pattern. She felt Steve was living a single lifestyle and wanted Steve's behavior to change or she would leave him.

Steve's close friend Jason was graduating from the police academy, and Steve wanted to attend his graduation. A number of Steve's high school buddies would also be attending. Mary did not want Steve to go because she thought Steve and his friends would drink excessively, and she didn't want to support her husband's drinking emotionally or financially.

This was a pivotal moment in their counseling. Mary threatened to end the relationship if Steve went on this trip. Steve insisted that he wanted to go and support his childhood friend.

In the past, Steve would call Mary controlling, and Mary would refer to Steve as an immature teenager. Since the marriage wasn't going to tolerate many more of these exchanges, it was crucial that Mary and Steve have a constructive dialogue about this decision.

Mary: You care more about your friends than you care about me.
Steve: That's not true. No one is more important to me than you and our daughter. I just feel loyal to Jason. He was very supportive to me during a time when I didn't get any support from my parents.
Mary: Well, now I would like to be the one who's supportive in your life.
Steve: I would like nothing more than that.

Finally they were talking about the real underlying issues that they could never access to when fighting. At our next meeting, Steve announced that he decided not to go to the graduation. Steve realized that it was more important to Mary that he did not go to the graduation than it was for him to go. He decided to make a stronger commitment to Mary. Steve was willing to give up some of his independence in order to strengthen his marriage. This dialogue was a turning point in their marriage.

People are typically kind to strangers. One often greets the delivery person, talks about the weather with the bank teller, makes small talk with the plumber, and is courteous at school meetings with other parents. However, when one comes home from a hard day of work, they can be short, grumpy, abrupt, and curt. People work diligently to be kind to people they don't know well but get sloppy when they walk through the front door. Before our meetings, Mary and Steve's conversations were certainly sloppy.

People say that strangers don't deserve to be treated in a disrespectful way. In a public arena, most people want to be perceived as being decent and kind, not as mean and rude. At home in the private arena, however, people give themselves permission to let the ugliness of their personalities emerge.

At work, someone is typically "on." They work hard at being respectful to their boss, decent to colleagues, and helpful to customers. Judgmental thoughts and feelings are typically restrained, because the consequences of unleashing them at work are high. Criticizing a boss or customer a few times could certainly be grounds for termination. However, when one comes home from work and criticizes their spouse for what a mess the house is, the person assumes their critical statements will not lead to a divorce. A spouse feels they can get away with critical statements at home.

People feel they can let their hair down and just be themselves at home. However, if spouses express their ugliness for long periods of time, it will have a detrimental effect on their relationship. Where a few inappropriate comments at work can get one fired, spouses will endure these comments for a much longer period of time because the commitment is so much deeper. Most people go into a marriage thinking that their spouse will be a partner for life. Unfortunately, they may take their partner for granted and allow their behavior at home to get careless.

Couples must have a higher standard when they converse with one another. Most clients in my practice say that their relationship with their spouse is much more important than their work relationships. So the goal for couples is to *treat one another more kindly than they would treat strangers or co-workers*. Our best behaviors should be displayed in our homes with the people we love. We can continue to treat strangers kindly; however, we should reserve our finest behaviors for the people we love the most.

Key Points

- Couples need to be vigilant about the words they use.

- Seek professional help if you need it.

- Treat spouses more kindly than strangers.

2

It's All in the Delivery

Meeting with a counseling professional who utilizes the divorce prevention strategies described in this book gives a couple opportunities to talk about issues that have created emotional barriers in their relationship. Initially in the work, some couples are unable to talk directly to each other. The history of hostility toward one another permeates the relationship. In order to avoid the repetition of hostility in the sessions, each spouse expresses his or her concerns directly to the professional. If the couple is to talk directly with each other, each partner needs to communicate without interrupting, criticizing, blaming, or being parental.

THE POWER OF WORDS

Although it is generally said, "actions speak louder than words," my experience is that words can have a powerful impact on the health of a relationship. In the following case example we see how words can undermine a marriage.

In my first session with Nancy and Ken, Ken complained that Nancy often criticized him, and Nancy said she could not help it. Nancy was very disappointed with her husband Ken. Nancy had been working long hours as a grocery store manager, and her husband Ken was floundering with his career. He would get jobs for brief periods of time but never seemed to hold on to them. Nancy was getting fed up. With two children at home, she felt that she was the primary breadwinner. Ken had recently gotten a new job, but it was based on commission with no salary. Nancy was threatening to leave Ken.

Ken felt terrible about himself. He wanted to contribute financially, but he just couldn't get his career on track. Nancy would refer to him as "loser" and a "free loader," which severely diminished his self-esteem as a husband and provider. Nancy's criticism could be relentless, and Ken began to believe that he was not capable of financially supporting his family.

Ken's previous history of leaving jobs and getting fired was embarrassing for him. He was once fired and never told Nancy, instead pretending to go off to work each day. He lied to her just to avoid ridicule. Once Nancy found out about his lying, her attacks became even more scathing.

In order to change this relationship pattern, I asked Nancy to stop her name-calling. I told Nancy that her criticism diminished Ken's self-esteem, which lowered his confidence to find work. Her role was to understand her husband's struggles rather than undermine him. She needed to provide support so they could figure out together how Ken could contribute more to the household.

Ken's dream was to be a comedian, but he didn't think he could make a living from it. Both he and Nancy agreed that he had great people skills. He just needed a way to make a living using these skills.

A good friend of Ken's was an administrator in a nursing home. The friend offered Ken a job providing care for elderly patients. Ken accepted the position, since he was interested in helping others. Although this wasn't the level of pay that he wanted to make in the long run, he thought he would be happy at what he was doing and could bring in a consistent income. A steady paycheck and a content husband temporarily satisfied Nancy.

Ken would ask Nancy not to put him down, but Nancy "couldn't help it." She was very angry about being the primary breadwinner. However, Nancy responded to the authority of a professional and attempted to follow my advice not to criticize her husband.

There was no way Ken was going to thrive unless he had Nancy's emotional support. When Nancy stopped criticizing him, he started talking about future plans. He decided to pursue a career in real estate. In this field, he was able to use his people skills and make more money. Nancy's abstaining from name-calling and her support of Ken allowed Ken to become a financial contributor.

The words that a couple uses to communicate can elevate or destroy their marriage. Most couples in distress have difficulty talking with one another about the issues that impact their lives, especially the hotter issues. They tend to blame, criticize, and force their points of view on their spouse. Couples need to create a safe environment, a place where they can share their points of view without being criticized or blamed. Then couples can talk comfortably about issues, ultimately transforming their relationship and their lives.

It is natural for couples to disagree with each other. We marry individuals with different values, opinions, thoughts, and ideas. These differences bring vibrancy to our relationships. It is inevitable that we will differ on how to raise our kids, handle money, divide chores, decide where to vacation, or what movie we see. These differences are not the problem. *The issue is how couples resolve these differences.* If issues are discussed in a respectful and supportive manner, the final decision can often be superior to the decision we would have made on our own.

The initial goal for couples is to eliminate fighting and negativity in the relationship. It is difficult to emotionally connect with someone towards whom we have strong negative feelings. Once a couple is able to reduce the level of negativity in their interactions, an emotional void between them often becomes apparent. At this point, couples can work toward redeveloping the emotional connection in their relationship.

Most individuals obtain their relationship skills from observing others, both in real life and the media. Initially we learn how couples interact by observing our parents. The problem is that a significant number of relationships provide us with poor role models. Rarely does one observe a healthy relationship when watching a movie.

Myths we have grown up with also dictate our relations. One common myth is that it is healthy for a couple to *fight*. However, it is rare for an out-of-control fight to be healing. In fact, the significant majority of fights are destructive to a relationship. What is accurate is that it is healthy to *disagree*. Since a relationship consists of two individuals with separate perceptions and opinions, it is normal to have disagreements. However, a fight takes place when that disagreement deteriorates into a form of verbal battle.

The reason for fights can sometimes seem silly. Couples can fight about the cap on the toothpaste, burned toast, or laundry on the floor. The subject of a fight is often unimportant. The issue is how a couple deals with their disagreements.

This doesn't mean a person should not be angry in a relationship. It is normal to experience anger at one's partner. How one expresses his or her anger makes the difference between having a useful dialogue and a fight that deteriorates into name-calling.

YOU DON'T HEAR ME

It is healthy for a couple to express their feelings skillfully to one another. In order to do this successfully, it is important for partners to communicate *one at a time.* If a husband and wife interrupts one another, the discussion typically shifts into a heated, unhealthy conflict in a relatively short period of time. In this situation, the recipient is less interested in listening than in interrupting to get his or her point across. This pattern can escalate into an unneeded conflict.

A pause in the conversation between speakers allows the discussion to maintain a relative degree of calm. The pause also increases the likelihood that the person who is not talking is listening. When a couple interrupts one another, the person who is not talking is often thinking about how to respond to their partner instead of just focusing on listening. It is very aggravating to be speaking and feel that one's partner is not listening. The speaker's tone becomes more emphatic in an attempt to be heard.

Partners need to learn how to recognize when it is their turn to speak. In typical conversations, there is a pause when the conversation moves from one speaker to the next. Some couples have a very difficult time recognizing this pause. Other couples ignore this pause. Sometimes a speaker will briefly pause to gather his or her thoughts. The listener must be able to recognize this as a "thoughtful pause" and allow the speaker to continue after gathering his or her thoughts.

An interruption is disrespectful. It is a common courtesy to let a person express him or herself until he or she comes to a natural conclusion. A partner with a history of interrupting is less skilled at recognizing when their significant other has finished getting across his or her point.

If a couple has difficulty recognizing the pause, the professional can initially have the speaker make a comment such as "I'm done" to indicate to the listener that they can respond. Although this is an awkward formality in conversation, it can initially teach a couple to recognize the pause. When a couple recognizes and respects the pause, the statement is no longer needed.

The professional can also inquire whether the speaker was actually finished speaking when the other partner begins. This also helps a couple to identify the pause.

If couples are allowed to speak over one another, the dialogue escalates very quickly and typically in a destructive way. Therefore *it is essential for couples not to interrupt one another*. When this rule is carefully enforced and practiced by couples, it allows couples to express themselves and feel heard.

ON THE ATTACK

Corrine and Bob had a very hostile relationship. Bob would frequently criticize and blame Corrine. Corrine would get so upset that she would stand up, hover over Bob, and use a tone of voice that was ear piercing. I could rarely have them talk directly to each other since it was so difficult for them to change how they interacted with one another.

Had I commented on every critical and blaming comment, I would have interrupted them virtually every statement. Therefore, I had all the conversations directed through me. If a spouse talks to me, I don't have to filter the criticism out of the statement since it is not said directly to their partner. This allows someone to express him or herself without having to filter their delivery. In the beginning of divorce prevention work, this can sometimes be a helpful way of getting the issues out on the table.

The first issues in the work tend to be the hottest issues. As the work proceeds, the issues become more lukewarm. As the couple progresses, their communication skills improve to the point where they can address issues with one another.

Corrine and Bob had an attractive nine-year-old daughter, Ashley, who was interested in modeling. A couple of years ago Ashley had pictures taken for her portfolio. Ashley had numerous auditions but had never landed a job. Since the previous photographs were a couple of years old, Corrine wanted to redo Ashley's modeling pictures. However, Corrine went back to the photographer without consulting Bob.

When Corrine told Bob what she had done, Bob was incensed. Since the previous pictures never landed Ashley a job, he questioned whether it was a good use of their money.

At this point, Corrine and Bob had made enough progress in their treatment to talk directly to each other about this specific issue. Bob told Corrine that he thought the decision to get photographs was "stupid." Because this was a critical comment, I had Bob redo this statement. It was important for Bob to learn how to transform critical statements into non-critical statements. Since Bob was not able to create a noncritical statement on his own, I demonstrated an alternative statement: "I don't think we should have invested additional money in the photographs."

Corrine typically would have responded defensively to Bob's critical statement. Faced with the alternative statement, however, Corrine was not defensive. She explained that she got a less elaborate version of the photographs for only half the price. She also paid the photographer from her personal bank account. Bob said that he was still upset that she didn't consult with him. Corrine agreed that she should have done so.

Normally this dialogue would have spun out of control very quickly. The typical pattern would have been as follows: Bob would have been critical, Corrine defensive, Bob would have made another critical or blaming statement, and Corrine would have started shouting at Bob. My intervention ensured that Bob didn't make a critical statement in the first place.

When the couple processed how the dialogue went, Bob said to Corrine, "You never said it to me that way before." Corrine then became defensive because Bob had focused on the negativity of Corrine's past statements instead of how positively the latest interaction had gone. The language and tone criticized Corrine's past performance rather than expressing appreciation for her current performance. Even after a successful interchange, this one statement could have easily escalated into a shouting match.

I suggested how to redo this statement: "I appreciate how clear you were with me." To further elaborate, if Bob had said, "I appreciate how clear you were with me *this time*," the small addition of the words "this time," would criticize Corrine for not being clear in the past. This is how subtle conflict can be. Just the addition of two words or a change in the tone of voice can make a supposedly supportive statement critical.

Criticism is probably the most destructive force in a relationship. Critical statements pound at the self-esteem of one's spouse. Critical statements are also a poor way of communicating one's point of view. The recipient of criticism will rarely agree with the criticism, and will most likely respond with defensiveness and criticism in return.

Ideally we want to be supportive and loving towards our spouses. We may disagree with their point of view or with how they behave. However, our role is to express our point of view without knocking at the integrity of our spouse.

It is OK to be angry in a relationship, but spouses should be aware of how they express that anger to each other. Anger *can* be expressed in a respectful and dignified manner. The role of the counseling professional is to teach spouses the skills of communicating anger and other feelings in this way.

Many individuals are not even aware that they are critical toward their spouse. Maybe they are expressing themselves as their parents did or as they observe other couples talking to each other. However, if an individual is not aware of his or her critical statements, it is essential that the professional make this person aware of this communication style.

Sometimes people will perceive a statement from their spouse as critical that the speaker states he or she did not intend to be critical. However, in my experience, if the recipient perceives a statement as critical, they are often correct. Even if a statement is actually not critical but is perceived as such, it is still problematic. The speaker still needs to redo the statement so that the point is made without the recipient feeling criticized. Without this change, the spouse may not hear the point; all they hear is the criticism.

To be successful negotiating differences, *communication needs to be noncritical.*

Critical levels

Criticism has different levels of intensity. Level one criticism is the most damaging. Level one criticism often involves name-calling. Swearing at a spouse is a clear example of a level one criticism. Calling a spouse "stupid" or "crazy" is also an example of this level. These statements attack the integrity of a person and are verbally abusive. Couples who use level one criticism have the highest degree of hostility. These couples' task is to eliminate these statements quickly.

Level one criticisms include those statements made intentionally to hurt one's spouse. Statements such as "I hate you" and "I never should have married you" serve no other purpose than to be cruel.

Level two criticism involves an individual commenting on a spouse's personality rather than their behavior. When an individual comments on a spouse's personality, they imply that a person always behaves in that manner. The skill in eliminating level two criticism is to comment on a spouse's behavior instead.

One example of level two criticism is referring to a spouse as "controlling." It implies that the person has a controlling personality and will always behave in this manner. The spouse may be *behaving* in a controlling fashion, for example, telling a spouse what to do. However, calling a spouse "controlling" labels the person's personality rather than commenting on the person's present behavior. The spouse can instead comment on the verbal behavior by saying, "Please don't tell me what to do."

Another example would be an individual telling their spouse specifically how to clean the stove. The spouse's response could be, "I don't like when you tell me how to do things." This statement communicates the individual's experience as opposed to criticizing the spouse for being controlling.

Other examples of level two criticism include calling a person a "slob," "lazy," "mean," "selfish," or "overly sensitive"—all references to a person's personality. These terms imply that a person always behaves in this way. So, rather than calling a person "a lazy slob," which labels a spouse's personality, the focus needs to be on the spouse's behavior. For example, one can say instead, "It bothers me when you leave your clothes on the floor. I would appreciate if you could put them in the hamper."

Level three criticism is a more subtle form of criticism. Rhetorical questions and sarcastic humor are two examples of level three criticism.

Rhetorical questions are critical statements put in the form of questions. For example, the question "Why do you spend so much time watching TV?" implies that a person spends an excessive amount of time watching TV. It contains a subtle criticism for doing so. An alternative statement could be "Rather than watching TV, I would like to do something together."

When an individual asks a question, it is important to decipher whether the question is a direct request for information (question of curiosity) or a disguised form of criticism (rhetorical question). For example, "Where are my socks?" could be a neutral request for information. However, it could also be a criticism if the tone of voice blames the spouse for being behind with the laundry. ("Where (the hell) are my socks?") In a case such as this, the tone of voice indicates whether the question is a question of curiosity or a rhetorical question.

Almost all questions can be put into a statement form. "So why the hell did you do that?"—which is critical—could be transformed into "I was upset when you ..."—which is noncritical.

Jan and Mark were in the process of renovating their house. They both have a habit of using rhetorical questions with one another. One conversation went like this:

Jan: We talked about you painting the dining room. Why isn't the dining room painted?

Mark: Do you think I am just sitting around the house?
Jan: What did you do all day?
Mark: Why are you such a nag?

You can sense the level of criticism within the rhetorical questions. I asked Jan and Mark to redo the conversation without rhetorical questions, and it went like this:

Jan: Mark, you said that you were going to paint the dining room, but it's still unpainted.
Mark: I was planning on doing it, but the toilet started overflowing. I needed to address that problem before we had a flooding problem.
Jan: I understand, but I wish you had told me about the change of plans.
Mark: That's fair enough.
Jan: I appreciate that you took care of the problem with the toilet. If you still have time to get to the painting, that would be great.
Mark: No problem. I can get it started this weekend.

Sarcastic statements are actually critical statements disguised in the form of humor. If someone is called a four-letter word by a person who cracks a big smile, does the recipient react to the word or to the smile? Most people would react to the four-letter word. The smile only lets the person get away with the name-calling.

The person being sarcastic typically thinks he or she is being funny. However, the recipient will typically experience some degree of criticism. The smile only tones down the intensity of the criticism.

Sarcasm may occasionally be funny when it is directed at people not present. However, sarcasm is not funny when it is directed at an individual, especially a spouse. An individual who uses sarcasm needs to use a different type of humor in their relationship.

IT'S YOUR FAULT

Paul and Stacy met in college. Despite Paul dating a number of different women, Stacy pursued him persistently. She was determined to be in a committed relationship with him. Eventually Paul stopped dating other woman and was monogamous with Stacy. However, he continued to spend a lot of time with friends. Stacy constantly felt like second fiddle. Stacy often demanded to spend more time with Paul, and Paul frequently distanced himself by spending time with friends. When they graduated from college, Stacy insisted on getting married. Paul eventually relented.

Stacy frequently expressed her anger at Paul. She often attacked him for spending too much time with his friends and not enough time with her. These attacks further alienated Paul. Paul's increased distance further incensed Stacy.

When I met Paul and Stacy, they had been married for a decade and had several children. During our work, one exchange went as follows:

Stacy: Paul, I am tired of your single lifestyle. You're not committed to this marriage. If things don't change, I'm going to end this marriage.
Paul: If you weren't so attacking, maybe I'd be around more.
Dr. Rein: Paul, your work is to make a greater commitment to your marriage than to your friendships. If you can do that, Stacy will be less angry. Stacy, your work is to express your upset without attacking. If you could do that, Paul could feel more committed. When you blame each other, it's hard for each of you to make the changes you need.

The majority of couples engaged in treatment blame each other for their problems. Their perception is "if my spouse was different, we wouldn't have these marital problems." Initially, most individuals hope to convince the professional of how their spouse is really the problem. The professional, however, must maintain neutrality. Marital conflict is rarely about who is right and who is wrong. Conflict is about dysfunctional communication patterns.

When one spouse makes a blaming statement, the other spouse typically makes a blaming statement in return. A conflict escalates very quickly when couple exchanges blaming statements: "It's your fault." "No it's not, it's your fault!"

Change only occurs within an individual. If one person behaves in a different but positive way, their spouse is almost required to behave differently in response. The old, negative pattern of interaction is thrown out of balance. However, if an individual demands that his or her spouse behave differently, it rarely changes the relationship pattern.

Because change occurs within the individual, it is possible to change marital patterns with only one person. However, it is typically more effective for both spouses to be present since the professional can potentially influence both spouses to make changes within themselves.

I versus you statements

An easy way to identify blaming statements is to notice that they often start with the word "you," e.g., "You are …" or "You always do…." These "you" statements put the focus on the other person. As previously stated, change does not occur if the focus is on the other person.

"I" statements put the focus back on the individual. "I" statements allow one to share their experience without blaming the other person. A useful structure for communicating an "I" statement is "I feel … when you…." Examples include "I feel upset when you call me stupid" or "I get angry when you scream at the kids." These "I" statements communicate an individual's reaction to his or her spouse's behavior. "I" statements communicate the impact a spouse's behavior has had on the person making the statement. This can be important feedback.

It is possible to make "you" statements that appear to be "I" statements. For example, "I think *you are a jerk*!" is actually a "you" statement. The actual statement is "You are a jerk" but the speaker attempts to cloak it as an "I" statement by putting "I think" in front of the "you" statement. One must be careful of this tendency.

YOU'RE NOT MY PARENT

Cindy was miserable in her relationship. Her husband Chuck was quite verbally abusive and very controlling. After years of being emotionally pounded, Cindy had become quite depressed and withdrawn. Her psychological health was deteriorating. Despite having young children, Chuck went off to graduate school in a nearby state. This allowed the couple to put off dealing with their marital issues. They coexisted, occasionally see-ing each other on the weekends. The couple sought out my services just before Chuck graduated from school.

The goal of the professional work was to draw Cindy out so that she could be more assertive with her husband. She had lost her voice in the relationship and needed to regain it. Her husband needed to severely tem-per his overpowering style and find less angry and forceful ways to express himself. This particular couple would have been very unlikely to resolve their differences on their own. A professional needed to change their inter-personal styles. In our meetings, Chuck became more vigilant of his ten-dency to tell Cindy what to do and how to do it. Cindy became more assertive and began to tell Chuck when she perceived him as being paren-tal.

Chuck and Cindy exhibit the importance of working on one's individ-ual issues in the context of a marriage. Chuck made an effort towards elim-inating his domineering and parental style. Cindy regained her voice and began to reassert herself in the relationship.

In addition to critical and blaming statements, parental statements are also harmful to a relationship. Parental statements are appropriate when said to a child, but are problematic when they are stated to an adult. There are three types of parental statements:

1. The Dictator—ordering or telling a spouse what to do or not do

2. The Professor—communicating that you are right and your spouse is wrong

3. The Psychoanalyst—stating your interpretation of why a spouse behaves the way that they do

Individuals are more likely to listen to people in positions of authority such as bosses, teachers, and doctors. These are hierarchical relationships; these individuals typically have more power or knowledge. One is more likely to do what they request, listen to what they have to say, or accept their understanding of a situation. A marriage is a relationship of equals. If one spouse tries to wield power or authority, it will typically be met with resentment.

The Dictator

Most people don't want to be told what to do, and this includes spouses. Dictators give their spouses direct orders or demands. "Do this;" "Don't do this;" "Straighten up after yourself;" "Wash the dishes;" "Do this chore." The dictator's error is not with the request; it is with the delivery.

Spouses like to be asked rather than be told. Some examples of requests, rather than orders, include "Would you mind taking out the garbage?" or "I'd appreciate if you could take out the garbage." Asking is respectful. It gives room for a spouse to negotiate: "I can take the garbage out after this TV show." It also gives one's spouse the option of saying no.

Again, the key to not being a dictator is to transform orders and demands into requests. "Do this" becomes "Would you mind ...?" or "I'd appreciate...."

The Professor

In the classroom, professors are typically a wealth of information. They have advanced degrees and are usually well-read in the area they are teaching. However, in the home, it is unappealing when a spouse insists that his or her information is always right.

It is OK for a spouse to give information to a husband or wife. However, it is important that the underlying dynamic is not, "I am smarter than you," "I am more knowledgeable than you," or "I am right and you are wrong." In these extremes, the person becomes a know-it-all.

Couples may disagree about what is true, and spouses may have contradictory information. However, a relationship is not helped when one constantly proves that he or she is superior. Having a healthy relationship is more important than being "right."

The Psychoanalyst

When someone tells their spouse why the spouse behaves the way he or she does, that person is playing the role of the psychoanalyst. One example of this is referencing a person's past: "The reason you ignore me is because your father never paid attention to your mother." Maybe there is some truth to this, and maybe there is not. However, when a spouse makes an analysis or interprets a spouse's behavior, the recipient typically resents it.

The psychoanalyst may analyze or interpret a patient's behavior, since this is a hierarchical relationship. The analyst has more authority than his or her patient. However, when a spouse does this to a husband or wife, it is often met with resentment. The husband or wife may think, "Who are you to tell me why I behave the way I do?"

The guideline is that spouses should not analyze each other's behavior, but instead tell their partner how a particular behavior impacts them. Analyzing one's spouse's behavior within the context of a marriage rarely creates behavior change. Analysis makes one spouse feel like the expert and makes the other spouse feel inferior. Behavior change is more likely to occur when a spouse gives direct feedback of how a certain behavior impacts him or her.

A former patient of mine worked in the publishing industry, an industry in which making deadlines is vital. He was very direct and authoritative with those under him. He would typically give them orders and make demands on them. He would take this authoritative style home, often telling his wife what to do. The wife obviously resented being ordered. He also played the professor role, insisting that he was always right. In addition, he played the psychoanalyst role, telling her why she behaved the way she did. This was a deadly combination of being the dictator, the professor, and the psychoanalyst.

THREE STRIKES, YOU'RE OUT!—THE POINT OF NO RETURN

Conflicts in relationships typically begin with an individual making a critical or blaming statement (strike one). The spouse receiving this statement will experience the statement as an attack. This spouse will typically respond to the attack by making a critical or blaming statement in return (strike two). If the initial person continues with a critical or blaming statement (strike three), it is very unlikely that the couple will be able to halt this pattern of mutual criticism and blame.

I refer to this third strike as the *point of no return*. Once the third statement of criticism or blame is made, it is very difficult for a couple to recover. After the point of no return, couples often make comments to one another that they do not mean and they may regret. Level three or level two criticism can become level one criticism (name-calling). Couples may even talk about divorcing or separating as a way of attacking each other. This "divorce talk" is very destructive because it shakes the foundation of the relationship.

The intervention needs to be at the first or second critical or blaming statement. It is easiest to intervene at the first statement. If a partner slips and makes such a statement, it is imperative for the recipient not to respond in kind. Intervening at this second statement is more challenging, since our natural tendency is to defend and then attack in return. The skill for the recipient is to filter through the criticism or blame and respond to the essence of the message. This is the moment at which a person needs to elevate him or herself not to respond in kind, thereby significantly reducing conflict.

Everything and the kitchen sink

Once couples reach the point of no return (the third attacking statement), anything can be said. This is the point when a conversation can spiral out of control. Couples begin to say things for the purpose of attacking and hurting each other. These statements are often verbally abusive.

When I review conflicts that escalate out of control, I concentrate on the need to stop the escalation early. Rarely are statements after the point of no return a reflection of someone's true feelings. Rather, they are simply attempts to hurt the other or to retaliate against a perceived hurt made to them.

Although I put little credence in the statements made after the point of no return, spouses will sometimes hold on to these statements as if this is what their spouse really thinks. But that is rarely the case. Statements such as "I really hate you!" "You are a ...!" "I never should have married you!" are typically attacking statements made in the heat of the moment, designed to have an impact.

The work is always to avoid these statements. They can be extremely detrimental to a relationship. If a couple can avoid going past the point of no return, they significantly increase the chances of success. If not, these verbally abusive statements take a tremendous emotional toll on the relationship.

The cold war

When a couple is in conflict, the interchanges may range from negative to hostile. However, a couple learns over time that they are not able to resolve particular issues with each other. Any attempt to do so is going to result in hostility. So rather than engage in another fruitless fight, the couple begins to withdraw from one another. They grow apart emotionally and begin to live parallel lives.

The marriage may revolve around maintaining the household or staying together for the sake of the kids. The couple is no longer remaining married because they feel in love with each other. It becomes a marriage of convenience. Maybe one partner fears the financial implications of two households or is embarrassed by failing at the marriage. Maybe one doesn't want to leave because they can't tolerate the thought of not seeing the kids everyday.

Rather than overt hostility, the couple emotionally pulls away from each other. This cold silence reflects the emotional abyss in the marriage.

This is a marriage at risk. Since couples can rarely resolve this cold war on their own, it is important that they seek professional intervention.

Key Points

In order to improve the delivery:

- Do not interrupt

- Eliminate criticism

- Stop blaming

3

Marital Themes

IT SEEMS SO MINOR BUT ...!

Minor irritations are a typical aspect of married life. Our spouses do things that irritate and annoy us. So how do we deal with these irritations?

Many people try to change their spouse's "annoying" behaviors by criticizing these behaviors. However, when an individual is criticized, this rarely motivates a person to change.

When couples talk to me about these small irritations, they often seem embarrassed by how minor the problems are. However, the issue is not how minor these irritations are; the issue is instead how a couple talks to each other about these minor problems.

Jan and Mark are a couple in their late forties who have been married for twenty-two years. Jan recently talked to me about minor irritations that had become an issue in her marriage. Her husband, Mark, had a history of being critical. Jan, in turn, had become quite withdrawn. In our first meeting, Jan made it clear that she was planning to divorce him unless the marital dynamics changed. Realizing their relationship was in peril, Mark became aware how much he loved his wife and was willing to do anything to save his marriage.

In the course of our sessions, Jan was learning to become more assertive, and Mark was improving his ability to listen and to be more responsive to his wife.

During one meeting, Jan expressed that she was irritated by some minor behaviors but felt embarrassed about mentioning them. I encouraged her to share these irritations, telling her that this would be an opportunity for her to assert herself. Mark would listen and, I hoped, be responsive. The conversation went as follows:

Jan: Don't you realize that I don't have a place to hang my clothes in the **bathroom?**

Dr. Rein: Jan, that statement is critical and blaming. Try expressing how **important** it is for you to have a place to hang your clothes in the bathroom.

Jan: I am angry that you didn't put a hook on the back of the bathroom **door like** you said you would. I need a place to hang my clothes.

Mark: Why don't you go out and buy the hook?

Dr. Rein: Mark, your comment is attacking. I want you to listen to Jan's request and attempt to be responsive.

Mark: OK. I didn't put the hook up because I wasn't aware of how important it was to you. I didn't know it was bothering you. I also didn't know what kind of hook you wanted. I figured we could go out shopping and pick out a hook together.

Jan: I don't care what kind of hook you put on the door. I only care that it is silver in color, to match the towel holders.

Mark: OK, I'll take care of it. If you wouldn't mind picking up the hook from the store when you are out, I'd be glad to hang it.

Jan: Great.

The issue wasn't with the hook. The issue was how this couple spoke to one another. Without professional intervention, this "minor irritation" could have easily spun out of control.

The other issue here is whether Jan should bring up the problem at all. Was Jan's irritation regarding the bathroom hook even worth bringing up? Sometimes certain pet peeves are not worth addressing. However, because Jan kept returning to how much this problem bothered her, she felt she needed to express herself.

After the hook incident, Jan proceeded to talk about other irritations she had with Mark. She didn't like that he left the sponge in the sink, that he left his hair products on the bathroom counter, and that he didn't put the toothpaste cap back on the toothpaste tube. These may seem like minor complaints, but Jan felt a need to express these irritations. Jan was able to express her pet peeves correctly, without criticism or blame. Mark was able to listen and said that he would make an effort to be more responsive to her concerns.

My hope for the couple is that Mark will continue to be responsive. However, he may not always be attentive to his wife's concerns in the future. If this is the case, it may have more to do with his personality. For example, he may be regularly distracted or unfocused, resulting in his inattention to these situations. Some people naturally clean up after themselves, while others tend to leave a trail behind them. This can be a personality issue that may be resistant to change.

In this case, since the marriage was at considerable risk, it was very important for Mark to make a real effort to respond to his wife's pet peeves. Mark had a long history of being unresponsive to his wife, and this was an opportunity for him to change this pattern. If he continued to be unresponsive to her concerns, it would put their marriage in jeopardy.

A minor irritation had also come between another couple with whom I worked. Lauren complained that Ed would leave the dirty bath water in the tub after his bath, rather than drain it. Previous attempts by the couple to talk about this issue just between the two of them had been unsuccessful. When Lauren and Ed described their previous conversations on this topic, the dialogue had been critical, defensive, and unproductive. They were now willing to discuss it with me there to guide them. In our session, Lauren expressed to Ed how his decision not to drain the tub irritated her:

Lauren: It annoys me when you don't drain the tub. I have to put my hand through dirty bath water to drain the tub and clean the ring of dirt left by the water in the bathtub.

Ed: My brother told me that after consuming energy to heat the hot water, it was good to leave the water in the tub to help with keeping the heat and humidity in the air on a cold winter day. He taught me that letting a large amount of hot water drain into the sewer system wasted energy because the water could otherwise serve as a heat source.

Because this conversation had never gone well in the past, Lauren had never heard these explanations. Despite the fact that Ed made a very good income, she was impressed that he would think in such an environmentally conscious way. She appreciated hearing this explanation, because it gave a context to what she initially perceived as being a very odd behavior. The couple found some middle ground on this issue. Ed could hear how putting her hand through dirty bath water bothered his wife. Lauren now understood her husband's rationale. Lauren agreed to tolerate the dirty bath water on cold winter days, and Ed agreed to drain the water when it wasn't cold out.

These couples were initially very reluctant to bring up these issues with me. They were embarrassed by how silly they appeared to be. Working through minor irritations in a relationship is essential. How these minor irritations are dealt with can either build a relationship or potentially blow a marriage apart.

WHAT DO YOU MEAN YOU CAN'T CHANGE?

Personality characteristics are typically enduring. However, a person's behavior can change. The distinction between the two—personality and behavior—is essential. One may have to tolerate a spouse's unattractive personality characteristics but can request that a spouse change his or her behavior. In order for expectations to be more realistic, it is important to distinguish between personality and behavior. Some personality characteristics that are less likely to change include the following:

1. Messy versus neat

2. Late versus punctual

3. More sensitive versus less sensitive

4. Reserved versus outgoing

5. Anxious versus calm

For example, an individual can express that he or she gets upset when their spouse comes home late for dinner (the late versus punctual characteristic). However, if this feeling is expressed constantly, the statement becomes nagging. Nagging is rarely effective in changing behaviors. It often encourages the recipient to attack back or to withdraw. The spouse making dinner has the right to express his or her feelings, but in a noncritical, nonblaming way. If the behavior doesn't change after two separate requests, the person may need to accept that he or she will have to adjust to the spouse frequently being late. Maybe he or she won't start cooking dinner until the spouse calls from the cell phone on the way home. Maybe the person eats without the spouse if he or she is not home by a certain time. Whatever choice is made, it is important that the decision eliminates nagging—excessive requests—and minimizes resentment. This, of course, means tolerating a personality characteristic that is unattractive. However, the alternative, to constantly nag a spouse to change, is typically an ineffective strategy.

Behaviors that are more likely to change are verbal behaviors—how spouses talk with one another. If a spouse is critical, the verbal behavior of criticism can be changed to noncritical statements. Blaming statements can be changed to nonblaming statements, such as "I" statements. Rather than accusing a person of having a critical or blaming personality, a spouse may point out when their partner speaks in a critical or blaming manner. The latter behavior is amenable to change.

Another behavior that can change is listening. A person can learn how to become a more skillful listener. However, there may be limits to how good of a listener a spouse can become. Personality characteristics, such as anxiety, sensitivity, and distractibility, can impede the level of listening ability.

Sensitivity is a personality characteristic. It is not a trait that is very amenable to change. When married to a sensitive person, the challenge is on the communicator. If one says, "You're too sensitive," the statement is considered critical. The communicator needs to learn to express comments more carefully to decrease negative reactions. This ability often requires developing a higher degree of communication skills. On the other hand, being married to a sensitive person can be beneficial, since that person is likely to be attuned to their partner's feelings.

A couple who I treat recently learned about this issue. The wife was not employed outside of the home, and her husband made an offhand comment about it. His wife felt criticized and mentioned it, to which her husband replied that she was "too sensitive." With my help, the husband was able to change his wording from a comment about her "sensitivity" to a statement about his concerns regarding the family's financial situation. This enabled the couple to talk more effectively about whether or not both of them should work.

You're not easy to live with

When we are dating, we rarely notice that our partner has flaws. We feel thrilled to find someone who is attractive and is equally attracted to us. We feel excitement when we are with this person. We want to spend a lot of time with this person and look forward to the next outing. We see the positive qualities in our partner, and ignore or minimize the less attractive qualities.

When we get married, less attractive qualities become more apparent or reveal themselves for the first time. We married the person because of his or her attractive qualities. If we think that we can change our spouses' unattractive qualities, we are mistaken. Behaviors can change, but people's personalities stay consistent. One of the skills of marriage is to tolerate these less attractive qualities.

FOUNDATIONS

Adam and Cheryl came to me because Adam suspected that Cheryl was having an affair. However, it became clear over time that this was not the case. Cheryl had very strong feelings for Adam and was not interested in straying outside the relationship. It appeared Adam's suspicions were unfounded and based on misperceptions.

Nonetheless, there were profound issues of trust in the relationship. Since Cheryl appeared unable to convince Adam that she was trustworthy, the focus of our work was to improve the emotional connection in the relationship. When couples have a strong emotional bond, spouses naturally trust one another. In a healthy marriage, it is unlikely that a partner would stray outside the relationship.

On closer examination, Adam and Cheryl had a communication style that created distance in their relationship. Adam had a tendency to communicate in a belittling tone. Cheryl frequently made demands on Adam and had high expectations of how she expected him to behave. When Adam didn't behave the way she expected, she could get quite demeaning herself.

The level of animosity and anger in this relationship was so strong that the couple could not talk directly to each other without constant criticism and blame. Therefore, communication was directed through me rather than them talking to each other. When the conversation is directed to me, one person speaks at a time with no interruptions. This allows each one to freely vent angry feelings.

Once enough anger is discharged, I allow the couple to talk directly to each other. It took a while for Adam and Cheryl to work through enough of their communication difficulties to be able to talk directly to each other about their problems.

This work was very challenging, since I needed to be constantly vigilant about how the couple talked with each other. The dialogue needed to move very slowly and deliberately. My job was to be sure that none of their direct communication was critical, blaming, parental, or analytical. If it was, I would point this out and either model how to make their statement in a healthier way or challenge them to do so themselves if I thought they were capable. When one of the spouses was critical, blaming, parental, or analytical, the recipient would almost always respond in a defensive way and have the tendency to attack back if allowed.

Since this pattern was going on at home for years, it was no wonder that the couple had many layers of issues unaddressed. They did not have a communication style that was going to allow them to work through their differences without professional intervention.

This couple actually had a very deep love for one another that I rarely see in couples. They both had a deep respect for each other. However, their communication style had become so destructive over a significant period of time that Adam thought his wife was having an affair. After one and a half years of diligent work, this couple learned how to communicate well with each other. They can talk about relationship issues and negotiate solutions without getting into conflict. Despite dealing with a major crisis, they became a strong support for each other.

This couple was honest with each other. However, one can see how unstable the foundation of a relationship can become even with the perception of dishonesty or infidelity. When a couple is actually dishonest or disloyal to one another, the foundation of the relationship can really tremble.

Healthy relationships cannot exist without honesty and fidelity. If one knows their partner doesn't always tell the truth, they can never know definitively whether anything he or she says is true. If one hasn't always been truthful, a basic premise of professional intervention is to be truthful beginning from this point forward.

Honesty is the foundation of any relationship. If someone has lied in the past, there will always be a question regarding their truthfulness. If the lie is recent, there is more reason to question the person's honesty. If the last time this person lied was five years ago, one may have a much stronger sense that this person is probably being honest this time.

If a person lies constantly, one expects statements from this person not to be truthful. If a person is inconsistent with their lying, one will never be sure. The bottom line is that if a partner is always truthful, his or her spouse doesn't have to question their integrity. Telling the truth also makes one more accountable for his or her behavior, since a person wants to minimize sharing uncomfortable or embarrassing information.

To make a commitment to a spouse, one must make a commitment to truthfulness. Does a person's truthfulness extend to telling a spouse that they have bad breath or what they are wearing looks terrible? In both these examples, making these statements would be considered critical. However, if a spouse asked how he or she looked, sensitivity mixed with honesty would be crucial to minimize conflict.

Fidelity is another form of honesty. During a wedding ceremony, two individuals make a vow to be faithful to each other. When a relationship is in distress, individuals tend to emotionally distance themselves from one another. Sometimes couples become so distant that they seek emotional connectedness through an affair. Affairs are rarely just about having sex. An affair is symptomatic of a relationship in significant distress.

Ideally a couple would seek treatment before an affair occurs. However, sometimes a sexual encounter or an affair is a wake-up call to a couple that they need professional help. Professional intervention can be challenging after an affair since the betrayal of fidelity is such a strong violation of honesty and integrity.

I once had the opportunity to work individually with a married man in treatment, who was considering pursuing a relationship with a woman he recently met. Fortunately I was able to discourage him from pursuing this relationship before it ever occurred. I explained to him that just the thought of pursuing this relationship indicated marital problems, and I encouraged him to address the marital issues before complicating his relationship with an affair.

I'D RATHER BE ALONE THAN BE MISERABLE

Occasionally, after working with a couple for a period of time, the professional will identify a relationship that is unlikely to change. Nonetheless, it is always up to each spouse to decide whether he or she is willing to tolerate a relationship being stuck. The couple is responsible for making this life-altering decision.

Some situations are less responsive to change. In these cases a decision to leave a relationship may be indicated. In cases of alcohol, drug, or physical abuse, a partner may find it necessary to leave if their spouse refuses treatment. Leaving a relationship might also be necessary if a spouse was having an ongoing affair and refused to stop.

Most other situations, while also difficult, are more responsive to change. For example, if a person stated that they wanted to leave a relationship because of the level of conflict, they might be advised that professional intervention can be quite effective for this problem. The professional work has a strong emphasis on eliminating negativity in the relationship. If a person wants to leave because they are no longer "in love" with their spouse, the goal is to reduce negativity and then work toward bringing emotional connectedness back into the relationship. It's hard to be in love with someone when he or she is constantly being mean. As the relationship dynamics change, the couple may experience the feeling of being in love again.

The couple will not be able to regain the "in love" feeling that they had during courtship. That level of intensity and passion is only characteristic of the first stage of relationships. Instead, we are looking for the steadier, more moderate feeling of love that is characteristic of mature, stable relationships.

In select situations, so much damage has been caused by negativity or distance over the years that the relationship is unable to recover. In such a relationship, if one spouse absolutely decides the relationship is over, then the marriage is over.

Key Points

- How couples address minor irritations is important.

- Spouses need to tolerate personality characteristics since they are unlikely to change.

- Honesty is essential for a healthy relationship.

4

Money, Sex & Kids

We have been talking about how to resolve conflict in a relationship. However, what are the problems that cause couples conflict? Often they relate to money, chores, children, extended families, and sex. This chapter talks about each of these areas—how they can be areas of potential conflict and how the conflict can be diminished.

YOU BOUGHT WHAT?

Ed made a decent living as a salesman, and Laura was a stay-at-home mom. Despite Ed's very good income, Laura and Ed often fought about money. Ed felt that Laura spent too much money on clothing and household items for the house. He felt Laura was being irresponsible about her spending, and Laura felt Ed was trying to control her. Their conflict about money had become a pattern of name-calling: Laura was irresponsible, and Ed was controlling.

My initial work with them was to talk about what they valued. Laura said that it was important for their kids to go to college, and she wanted to be able to fund this for them. Ed agreed and said that it was also important for them to retire at a reasonable age with a reasonable income. Laura agreed with this. It was also important that the family vacation together so the family could have memorable moments together. However, this goal was not as crucial as education and retirement.

Since Ed was the bookkeeper for the family, I asked him to bring in a budget. We wanted to examine together how much income was coming in and where the money was going. Our goal was to create a budget that reflected their joint family values.

The budget revealed that they were saving relatively little money for education and retirement. Despite how important these values were to Ed and Laura, their budget did not reflect these values. They did observe that a significant amount of money was going towards vacations, eating out, clothing, and household items.

As we made this discovery, I stopped Ed when he began to make the statement "I told you so." The numbers spoke for themselves, and Laura was quick to recognize that they needed to change how they spent their money. Since the kids were approaching middle school age, she decided to get a part-time job in a clothing store. She would fund her desire for nice clothes through this job, and at a discounted employee rate. She would also use the money from this job to buy items for the house. Ed talked about eating out less frequently as a family. Ed also talked about being careful about how many vacations they went on per year and to be vigilant about how much money they spent on a particular vacation.

Laura and Ed redid their budget. They were both determined to reallocate the money for vacations, eating out, clothing, and household items towards education and retirement. Laura and Ed felt empowered that they were finally working as a team for the best interest of the family.

Finances are the number one stressor in relationships. Money represents survival in today's society. We need money to survive. When a couple experiences more money going out than income coming in, it can have a very stressful impact on a relationship. When couples disagree about how they are spending their money, it can also have a detrimental effect on the relationship.

When these situations occur, couples tend to blame each other for spending too much or not making enough. It is not unusual for one spouse to be more of a spender and the other spouse to be more of a saver. Overall, this is not a bad difference to have. One person wants to create future stability and save for the future. The other person wants to spend money and enjoy life in the moment. The problem comes when these two distinct styles grate against each other.

In a perfect world, a person would have a fine balance between spending and saving—living for the moment and saving for the future. Unfortunately, this type of person is in the minority. However, if the spender and saver in a relationship can work in a coordinated fashion, they can create a balance of enjoying life and future stability.

The key is to have the spender recognize the benefits of saving for the future and to have the saver allocate some resources to the enjoyment of life. Many Americans do not live within their means. A couple's challenge is to work as a team and live within their means.

Many couples have a tendency to spend money independently. If a guy wants a car or motorcycle, sometimes he goes out and buys one. If a woman wants expensive clothing, she goes out and buys it. However, it is very important for a couple not to make large expenditures independently. Partners need to consult with one another when a purchase goes above an agreed upon amount.

Partners need to decide together how they want to spend their limited financial resources. For example, John wants to go out and buy a motorcycle. However, his wife Gloria wants to spend money on a Caribbean vacation. If John goes out and purchases this motorcycle on his own, he is likely to have a very angry spouse. However, if John expresses to his wife how important a motorcycle is to him, and Gloria expresses the importance of the vacation, they can develop a plan together that is responsive to their desires and is also fiscally responsible.

How a couple spends money demonstrates what they value. If one couple spends money on vacations and cars, this reflects their values. If another couple saves for retirement and the kids' education, this also reflects their values. When a couple is struggling with financial issues, it is important for the couple to share what their values are with each other and look for common values. A couple's budget would ideally reflect these shared values.

Couples are expected to have different values, but the skill is to find commonality even with their differences. Once a couple discovers these shared values, the next step for the couple is to create a budget that reflects these values. Is it saving for a nice home or addition or is it saving for the children's education?

Many couples struggle financially and live paycheck to paycheck. This allows a couple to survive; however, it doesn't allow them to plan for the future. It can be helpful for a couple to be aware of what income comes in per month and then track how the money is being spent.

A couple with no budget can take several months to track money and assess how money is being spent. Once the partners see how much is coming in and where it is going, they can start making joint decisions about how to spend their money. If a couple finds that more money is going out than coming in, they can decide how to reduce expenses or bring in more income. It is essential for couples to work as a team in order to change their financial situation. Blame is not an effective technique.

A couple can design their budget to reflect their shared values. For example, a couple finds that they are spending two hundred dollars a month eating out. They also find that no money is being saved for the children's college education. This budget demonstrates that their spending habits may be out of line with their values.

Despite enjoying eating out as a family, they decide to have a great dinner at home on Sunday nights and limit their eating out budget. They take the one hundred dollars they save per month and redistribute it to a college fund. When looking at their budget, the couple saw that they were putting a higher value on eating out than saving for their children's education. With this one shift, the couple began working as a team to begin saving for their children's education.

The majority of couples have joint budgets (although some couples have separate accounts early in a marriage.) A well-run joint budget reflects a couple that is working as a team to maintain and grow a household. Separate budgets reflect couples with more individualistic styles. However, some couples need separate accounts to work more like a team.

In a relationship between a spender and a saver, a couple may need separate accounts. For example, the saver's budget could focus on savings or paying for fixed expenses, such as the mortgage and utilities. In contrast, the spender could be given a budget of an agreed upon amount to be spent on discretionary items. This allows the saver to be less vigilant about how the spender spends the money. This also gives the spender more freedom to spend however he or she wishes, although he or she will still be required to live within that budget.

Some couples have difficulty with budgeting. It can be time consuming, and some people find tracking money onerous. Instead, a couple may decide that they want to commit to a particular value. For example, they may put a certain amount of money or a percentage of income into the children's college education every month. This is more likely to happen if it is the first check written each month. This is even more likely to happen if the amount is automatically withdrawn into a separate savings or investment account.

Financial stress can have a very deleterious effect on a marriage. How a couple discusses finances can range from hostile—when a couple is fighting—to invigorating—when a couple is working together for their future. The goal is to have a couple working as a team and to have the couple's spending and saving habits aligned with their joint values.

I DO EVERYTHING

Chores make a household function. In order for a family to be sustained, someone has to shop for food, clean clothes, and repair the house and cars. When we are single, we do it all. When we are married, there is a distribution of labor.

In most households, the majority of chores tend to fall on the woman. Until the middle of the last century, men were typically the breadwinners, and women stayed at home with the children. This history still influences today's American families. In a traditional household, the husband works full time and the wife stays at home with the children. In a dual-income family in which both the husband and wife work full time, the division of household labor needs to be more evenly balanced. However, research demonstrates that even in a dual-income family, women do seventy percent of the chores (Gottman and Silver 2000).

Whether we work in an office full time or in the home full time, chores are often one of our least favorite tasks. In order to have an efficient running household, the division of labor needs to be clear. Who does what chores? Who pays the bills, cleans the dishes, and helps with the kids' homework?

When a couple isn't clear about who does what chores, each often expects the other person to do a chore. If a couple attempts to share a particular chore, it often does not work well. Individuals get annoyed when their spouse is not doing what "they are supposed to be doing."

Sometimes couples need to make a list of chores in the household and decide who does what chore. So who is vacuuming the floor, cleaning the stove, or getting the kids ready for school? It is also important to clearly define what the chore consists of and how frequently the chore has to be done. Then it is up to the spouse to complete the chore. If a couple has the financial means, sometimes they can hire others to do some of the chores, such as house cleaning or lawn mowing. In today's world you can order your groceries online and have them delivered to your door. Unfortunately, most people can't hire someone to straighten up after a spouse or kids everyday.

It is typical for many couples to have different tolerance levels for messiness. It is not unusual to have one spouse who is neat and another spouse who is messy. When a neat spouse insists that a messy spouse be neat, this can be a recipe for trouble. Whether someone is neat or messy is typically a personality characteristic. Whether someone grew up in a neat or messy household could also be an influence. A neat spouse could spend years nagging a messy spouse to straighten up after him or herself and "the problem" remains. However, the real problem is that the neat spouse needs to take another approach besides nagging.

Neat spouses would prefer that messy spouses become neat like them. The first issue to recognize is that messiness is a personality characteristic that will not likely change. This is not to say that the messy spouse abdicates responsibility. However, the neat person needs to acknowledge that neatness is his or her value and may not be the spouse's value.

So what is a neat person to do? Well, one of his or her chores could be straightening. He or she can go through each room in the house and put items away. He or she can put the spouse's shoes in the closet and the spouse's clothes in the hamper. Often parents decide to have kids straighten up after themselves. However, when we attempt to do this with our spouses, we are treating them in a parental way and resentment results.

Remember that the goal of chores is to run an efficient household. The couple needs to be clear about who does what chores and that the division of labor feels fair. When a couple goes through the list of chores, I encourage couples to pick chores that they would not mind doing. I also have them express which chores they really dislike doing. It is in nobody's interest to have a spouse do a chore that he or she despises. If both spouses hate doing a particular chore, they can decide if they have the means to hire someone else to do the chore for them.

Another complaint that couples communicate regarding chores is not being complimented for doing their chores. I typically encourage couples not to expect compliments for chores. Chores are tasks that need to be completed in order for a family to function well. If it is in your heart to compliment a spouse for a job well done, by all means. If one expects to be complimented for how well the toilet was cleaned, they are setting themselves up for disappointment.

Chores bring up the issues of fairness and power in a relationship. When a household is running well, the distribution of chores feels equitable. The issue of power emerges when couples are not negotiating well and attempt to use their power to force their spouse to do a particular chore. This often creates resentment or passive-aggressive behavior: "I said I would do that chore, but I really won't." Good negotiation skills are necessary in order to decide upon chores.

Although a couple may make an agreement regarding chores, the husband and wife need to be aware that these agreements will change. It is possible that the initial agreement will need to be renegotiated immediately. Maybe a spouse realized that he or she hates doing a particular chore or was going to do a chore but never seemed to get around to it. In this case, it is important to make adjustments to the initial agreement. Both spouses need to feel comfortable with the amended agreement and that they can follow through on the agreement. When a spouse makes an agreement, follow-through is essential. If you don't follow through on the agreement, you lose trustworthiness—your spouse can't trust that you are going to do what you say.

Agreements on chores also need to be amended over time. A couple needs to renegotiate at various developmental stages in their relationship. For example, when a couple has a child their roles will change. Therefore, the chores will need to be rebalanced. Rebalancing may also occur when a spouse who is not working or is working part time significantly increases his or her work hours.

In summary, the goal for a couple is to be able to negotiate the division of chores equitably. The goal is to have a smoothly running household.

MY KIDS

Differences regarding parenting can be a major source of conflict in a relationship. The purpose of this section is to present a common parenting philosophy so parents can work in a coordinated, aligned fashion. If parents are working as a team, parenting differences are much less likely to create conflict in their relationship, and their kids will become better citizens as a result.

It is not unusual for parents to have different parenting styles. More often than not, these differences fall along the male-female divide. Men tend to focus more on being the disciplinarian, and women tend to focus more on being the emotional caretakers. However, there are plenty of families with female disciplinarians and male caretakers.

A common parenting pattern is to have one parent who is perceived as disciplining the children too harshly (the disciplinarian), and the other parent is perceived as being too lenient (the emotional caretaker). The disciplinarian feels their spouse is too easy on the kids, and they need to compensate by being firmer. The emotional caretaker thinks their spouse is being too harsh, and they need to compensate by giving the kids additional emotional support. This pattern typically continues and intensifies over time.

The goal for a couple is to balance their parenting styles. It is important for each parent to have a fine balance between being able to connect with their kids and being able to be firm with their kids. The parent who emphasizes discipline needs to strengthen their relationship with his or her children. The parent who emphasizes the relationship needs to be firm with the children and discipline them when appropriate. If the disciplinarian is less harsh, it gives room for the emotional caretaker to be firmer when needed. If the emotional caretaker is more active in the disciplinarian role, it gives room for the disciplinarian to improve their relationship with the kids.

The purpose of parenting is not to punish, nor is it to be friends with one's children. The purpose of parenting is to teach life skills to children. The goal is to teach kids how to become good, ethical people who are happy and can eventually give back to the world. If we can do this as parents, we have been successful.

As our kids grow, so does our parenting

When children are young, we begin to teach them about right and wrong. We praise our kids when they behave appropriately so that they are more likely to behave this way in the future. When our children behave inappropriately we often use consequences to teach our kids not to repeat that behavior. We also talk with our children about right and wrong.

Two and three year olds developmentally defy their parents. After being so dependent on their parents as infants, toddlers need to form their own identities. Toddlers separate themselves from their parents by saying no. It is important for parents to expect this as a necessary developmental stage for children. When we expect toddlers to behave defiantly, it is easier to emotionally detach from these behaviors. Their defiance isn't personal; it's developmental.

Parents need to pick and choose their battles during this developmental stage. Parents will certainly intervene if there are safety issues. If a toddler is going to touch an electric outlet, parents are going to intervene. If a toddler is refusing to get dressed for a pediatrician's appointment, a parent will dress them against their will and scoot them into the car. However, if the child wants to wear plaid pants with a striped shirt, parents could probably detach from this battle.

As toddlers become preschoolers, parents begin to use consequences to teach kids about right and wrong. The most common consequence is a time-out. A time-out happens when a parent puts a child in an isolated area for a certain period of time for behaving inappropriately. Because a time-out is a relatively easy discipline technique, a parent can use it every time a child behaves in an inappropriate manner. A standard amount of time for a time-out is either five minutes or a minute for each year of a child's age.

When parents use time-outs, they must be consistent in using the technique. One standard is to use time-outs when a child is defiant. A typical expectation is that when a parent asks a child to do something, the child complies. It is not necessary for a parent to make a request several times. It is also not appropriate for a parent to expect the child do the task at that exact moment.

A parent makes a request, and the child has twenty seconds to comply. If the child doesn't comply, then the parent warns them that if they do not do as they were told, they will be going into time-out. Usually the warning is enough to get the child to mind. If not, the parent escorts the child into time-out. Time-out typically works best in an isolated room such as a bathroom. Time-out in a bedroom can reward the misbehavior since most kids have games and toys in their bedrooms. Any talking back or defiance about going to time-out can be addressed by adding an extra minute for each offense. If the child makes a mess in the room they are put in, the natural consequence would be to have them clean up the mess after the time-out.

Although time-out is primarily used when a parent makes a request and the child does not comply, it can also be used to address specific behaviors such as fighting. If siblings fight, it is important that both children be put into time-out. In my observations of families, the younger or less physically strong child will often instigate fights, and the older child often responds by hitting. Since parents typically do not observe fights, parents need to assume that the younger child is also responsible. Therefore, both children should be put in time out.

Stopping a fight only requires that one individual walk away. If both kids are put into time-out, there is more incentive for each child to walk away from a fight later.

A fight is defined as one of the kids is crying because of an altercation or one of the kids says there was a fight. Since fighting is such a serious rule violation, I typically recommend doubling the time typically spent in time-out for other offenses.

When using time-out, it is important for parents not to lose sight of its purpose. It is used to teach children to comply with a parent's request and to teach conflict resolution (so children are less likely to resort to physical fighting). It is also important that a parent's requests are reasonable. If children are watching TV and left a toy on the floor, it would be more reasonable to request that the child pick up the toy during a commercial than to demand they do it immediately. The purpose of time-out is not to wield power over children but to empower parents in their negotiations with children. We are not trying to teach children who the boss is. We are trying to teach them life skills, such as cleaning up after themselves.

As kids move into latency age (about eight or nine), time-out begins to lose some effectiveness. This is a time when parents can move to using more of a teaching style to instruct their children about life skills. At this age, kids generally know the difference between right and wrong. The issue is how they choose to behave. This is when our parenting approach can involve talking with kids about doing the right thing and encouraging them to make good decisions. This is a good time to work on strengthening our relationship with our children. The stronger the relationship we have with our kids, the more influence we will have to help them make good decisions. When a parent uses a severe disciplinarian approach, the relationship deteriorates with the kids. This gives a parent less influence over time.

Parenting style becomes even more important as kids move into preadolescence and adolescence. This is a time when kids will naturally defy their parents. Not unlike the toddler stage, kids go through a deeper level of finding their identities and, therefore, asserting their independence. This is a time when parents may have a tendency to resort to a stricter disciplinarian approach. However, this is really a time when a parent needs to rely on the strength of their relationship and influence their teenager to make good decisions. I find the most frequent age for this transition is twelve for girls and thirteen for boys.

Our goal as parents is to create happy individuals who make good decisions. At this age, kids will be more influenced by their peers and the media than by their parents. However, we want to use whatever positive influence we have to keep kids from becoming involved with alcohol and/ or drugs or illegal activities. We want them to perform adequately in school and to make smart decisions about their safety. We can talk with them about their friends, peer pressure to use drugs and alcohol, and the importance of school for future success.

Discipline has limited influence at this age. Lecturing isn't helpful, since kids typically tune out lectures. However, a parent can still use natural consequences. If a child is late for curfew, he or she may need to come home earlier the next night. If a kid abuses phone privileges, he or she may lose phone privileges for a certain period of time. Fighting over computer time means the children do not get to use the computer for a brief period of time. If a kid is grounded for a serious rule violation, such as staying out all night, a week is typically considered the maximum consequence. Grounding consists of being confined to the house, often without the use of technology or electronics.

It is important that parents do not use denial of attendance at social events, such as school dances or sporting events, as a consequence for misbehavior. Because these events occur randomly, we can't use them consistently as consequences. In addition, we want to support the social and athletic lives of our children.

"Clean your room!"

Yelling at children is frequently seen in families. Parents yell for several reasons. First of all, parents use yelling to get children to comply with their requests. Secondly, parents use yelling as a form of punishment. Let's take a look at each of these and the effectiveness of yelling in each situation.

When parents make a request and children don't comply, parents may yell as a way of getting a child to comply. When parents make requests of children, they are asking children to do things that the children are not ordinarily interested in doing. Having a clean house may be important to an adult, but is rarely important to a child.

Parents may need to increase the volume of their voices to indicate the importance of a child complying with their request; however, parents rarely need to raise their voices to the point of yelling to get children to comply. Typically the issue is the physical distance between the child and the parent when the parent makes the request. For example, if a parent is right in front of a child and makes a request, the volume of the parent's voice does not need to be loud. However, if the parent is a distance from the child when they make a request, the parent's volume needs to be louder.

For example, let's say a parent wants their children to clean their playroom. A parent is downstairs watching TV and screams upstairs "Clean your playroom." The likelihood of this request being followed is extremely small and would only be carried out by an unusually compliant child. Also, the child does not take this request seriously since the request is being shouted from a distance. If cleaning the playroom is really important to the parent, the parent needs to walk up the stairs and make the request directly in front of the children. In addition, if the parent leaves at this point to return to the TV, the likelihood of the children complying with this request goes down significantly. If a parent wants the playroom straightened, the parent is required to stay in the playroom and watch the kids straighten it. Depending on the age of the kids, the parent may need to participate or provide organizational direction in straightening the playroom.

When a parent is making a request at a distance, the likelihood of compliance is low. Yelling is often indicative that the parent is communicating at a distance. One technique that is very effective for getting a child to comply is called the *Whispering Technique*. I discovered this technique in my relationship with my own kids. Rather than making a parental request from a distance, a parent makes the request by putting their face inches from the child's face, making eye contact with the child, and softly making the request, e.g., "I want you to clean the playroom." This request has to be made softly; otherwise the parent would be screaming in the kid's face, which would border on verbal abusiveness. The close proximity of the request and eye contact lets the child know that you are serious about the request. An elevated voice is unnecessary. If a parent has a decent relationship with their child, it is unusual for a child not to be compliant. Once again, the parent needs to stay in the presence of the child until the request is fulfilled.

Adolescents are notorious for messy bedrooms. Parents often talk about how there is barely a path from the teenager's door to the bed. How a teenager keeps his or her room is often a power battle between a parent's need for order and a teenager's assertion of independence. Similarly to interacting with a three-year-old, a parent needs to decide whether to take this battle on. If a parent is dealing with much larger and more important battles, I advise parents to concede. A parent can decide instead just to have the teenager keep his or her door closed. However, if order is a value that a parent wants to impart, then a parent may decide to confront this issue.

In summary, if a parent is making a request from a physical distance, the parent will have to yell their order. However, if the parent is making a request from close proximity, the parent can virtually whisper their request and get a much higher compliance rate. The likelihood of compliance is not correlated with the volume of the voice but with the level of connection that one makes with their child.

Parents also resort to yelling as a consequence for misbehavior rather than use time-out or natural consequences. However, yelling has a deleterious effect on the parenting relationship. Nobody likes when someone yells at them. Parents don't appreciate if someone yells at them at work for poor performance or mistakes. We would prefer if our bosses talked with us about how to improve our performance or decrease the likelihood of future mistakes, in other words, if they used mistakes as learning opportunities.

Yelling can be indicative of parents who are feeling out of control with their parenting. When parents feel somewhat ineffective, they often resort to yelling. Typically, time-outs and the whispering technique are more effective.

I didn't do it

One of the more serious violations for children is lying. We want to be sure that our kids tell us the truth.

Kids have a tendency to lie to get out of trouble. Because of this, it is important not to punish children when they tell you the truth. Otherwise, we end up punishing our kids for telling the truth.

If a child does something inappropriate and tells the truth about it, it can be a learning moment. We can talk with the child about how to behave differently or how to make a better decision in the future. We want to look for these opportunities to teach our children about doing the right thing. This has a more lasting impact on a child than grounding them for a day.

For example, a parent finds a broken window and asks his or her kids who broke it. The tendency for kids is to lie because they know telling the truth would result in paying for the window or getting some form of punishment. A parent wants to create an environment where telling the truth is supported. Breaking a window is usually an accident, and accidents are a part of life. Our goal is to learn from our accidents and mistakes, and we want our children to do the same. If a window is broken, we can talk with them about making better decisions about where to throw a ball. In the rare instance that he or she broke the window on purpose, then we would certainly want to understand what the child was feeling that would cause him or her to behave that way. Of course, if windows were broken repeatedly, a parent would need to consider consequences. If you have a decent relationship with your child, a discussion about the broken window and encouragement to tell the truth is more effective than a punishment.

OUTLAWS & EXES

Relationships between two people are complex enough. They become even more so when additional parties are added to the mix. One group that can negatively influence a couple is the in-laws. If the in-laws respect the boundaries of a couple's relationship and do not intrude on their parenting decisions, it is less likely that problems will occur. However, if the in-laws expect their children to take their side rather than their spouse's, problems will occur. Problems will also arise if in-laws interfere with parenting decisions.

In a healthy marriage, the relationship between the couple takes precedence over the relationship with one's parents. Couples need to work together not to allow the in-laws' influence to interfere with the marriage or the parenting relationship. Couples can be sensitive to the needs of their parents; however, the marital relationship is primary.

Sometimes a person can be pulled in different directions by a spouse and parents. If this is the case, the couple needs to strategize how to approach the parents. If one spouse follows the advice of his or her parents, without consulting their partner, marital problems are likely to ensue.

I worked with a couple in which the husband Jim had a close relationship with his widowed father. The wife, Kathy, was envious of the emotional closeness in this relationship, especially since their marital problems created so much emotional distance between them.

The goal was to eliminate negativity in the marital relationship in order to recapture emotional closeness. The focus was not on changing Jim's relationship with his father. He was entitled to have a close relationship with his father. However, the couple needed to strengthen their relationship so the father-son relationship was not so threatening.

When Jim's relationship with his father took precedence over the marital relationship, the couple experienced marital conflict. For example, Jim would leave the house and not tell Kathy where he was going. Jim was spending time with his father but was afraid to tell Kathy because her reaction was so negative. Kathy became even more enraged since her husband was being secretive.

Jim needed to consult with Kathy when he was going to spend time with his father. In addition, Kathy needed to temper her negative reaction when Jim made the request to spend time with his father. The work helped Jim to be more assertive and helped Kathy to respond without animosity.

Another in-law problem occurs when grandparents interfere with the couple's parenting. When the in-laws allow the grandchildren to disobey the parents' rules, the grandparents sabotage the parents' power.

For example, the Smiths have a rule of no eating in the family room. The kids, the parents, and the grandparents are all sitting in the family room watching a show together. While in the kitchen, one of the kids asks grandma if it is OK to have a Popsicle in the family room, and grandma says OK. When the kid returns to the family room with the Popsicle, mom asks, "What are you doing with food in the family room?" Grandma responds, "Don't be so uptight about eating in the family room." Grandma then says to the kids, "It's OK to eat in the family room."

This would be a clear example of parental sabotage. It is not OK for a grandparent to overrule the parents in front of the kids. This undermines parents and gives more power to the grandparents. In a healthy family structure, the parents have more power than the grandparents.

The previous example is blatant in order to illustrate the point. However, if grandparents sabotage the parenting in more subtle ways, it is important for the parents to present a united front and confront the grandparents. It would also be important for this discussion to occur out of the sight and earshot of the kids.

If grandparents are babysitting and they decide to let the kids eat in the family room, this is a different scenario. If grandparents know the house rule, they are disrespecting the parents. In this case, the parents can request that the grandparents respect the rule. However, if the grandparents continue to allow the kids to eat in the family room when they babysit, the kids will learn that it is OK to eat in the family room when just the grandparents are around, and it is not OK to eat in the family room when the parents are around. Although this is not ideal, most kids, even younger children, can make this distinction.

Another example is when the grandparents buy the grandchildren a lot of gifts. If the parents are more restrictive about gift giving because they "don't want to spoil the kids," they may request that the grandparents not be so lavish. However, the grandparents may want to shower the grandchildren with gifts since, as one grandparent once told me, "It is a grandparent's prerogative to spoil their grandchildren." If the grandparents continue to be overly generous, the children will need to distinguish between the gift-giving of parents and that of grandparents.

Some of the themes in dealing with in-laws are similar to the themes in dealing with ex-spouses. In a divorced family, kids will spend time in two different households with two separate sets of rules. It is ideal if the rules in both households are somewhat aligned. However, if one parent wants the rules in both homes to be aligned, rarely does an ex-spouse change his or her house rules to accommodate their ex.

If the two sets of household rules are very different, the kids learn to behave a certain way in one household and another way in the other household. However, if one parent were to tell their children that they did not have to follow the rules in the other household, this would be sabotage. A vengeful ex-spouse may feel like doing this, but it would be at the emotional expense of the children.

A divorced parent should never tell the children not to listen to their other parent. If one has an issue with the ex's parenting, the parent should address the issue directly with the ex-spouse. However, the parent needs to be careful not to criticize their ex. Ex-spouses are not typically receptive audiences. If a particular parenting approach is adversely affecting a child, the parent can talk with the ex about how he or she perceives the child as being negatively impacted. If this conversation is not effective and the issues significantly affect the children, professional intervention is a possibility.

Similar to the issue with in-laws, the relationship between a husband and wife always takes precedence over the relationship with ex-spouses. If an ex-spouse has an issue regarding a child, it is important that the remarried couple always work together as a team to address the concern. The couple needs to strategize how to deal with the ex and to ally with one another in dealing with the ex. Otherwise the ex will have a negative influence on the marriage. Dealing with a bitter ex-spouse can be stressful to a marriage, but if the remarried couple works closely with each other, these stresses can be minimized.

ANOTHER HEADACHE?

Sex is a wonderful way for a couple to be emotionally intimate with one another. When a couple is sexual, they are very vulnerable with one another. When sex is at its best, it allows a couple to express deep love and affection. So when a couple has significant marital problems, it shouldn't come as a great surprise that the vulnerability and emotional intimacy of sex are negatively affected.

Sex is an area in which the male-female differences are often pronounced. In general, when women feel emotionally close or intimate with someone, sex is a wonderful way to express those deep, loving feelings. In my conversations with men, it is less important for men to feel emotionally intimate to be sexual. However, sex may allow men to experience emotional intimacy with their partner.

This sex difference intensifies during marital problems. Men can experience their spouses as being distant and want to have sex as a way of getting emotionally close. Women are less likely to want to be physically close with someone with whom they are not feeling emotionally intimate.

Ruth was feeling very distant from her husband Dennis. He seemed to be tired all the time due to his overnight shift at work, and he was not very attentive to her. However, Dennis didn't have many complaints about Ruth. She was a good mother and attentive to his needs. His only complaint was the lack of sex in his marriage. He would frequently pursue his wife for sexual affection, but Ruth didn't want to have anything to do with Dennis physically.

Ruth also struggled to connect with Dennis emotionally. She perceived him as constantly pawing at her, looking to be physically affectionate. Dennis became sexually frustrated and tried even harder to get Ruth to submit. This just annoyed Ruth even more and made her less likely to want to be with him physically.

My professional role was to insist that Dennis stop pursuing Ruth in this way. The focus needed to be on their emotional connection with each other. If I could help them to emotionally connect, I hoped that the physical intimacy would eventually follow. Dennis's pawing pushed his wife further away. He needed to learn to talk to her and connect with her in other ways until Ruth was ready to pursue him physically.

Sex is indicative of the emotional health of a marriage. When a marriage is healthy and vibrant, a couple's sexual life continues to be exciting. When a marriage is suffering, a couple's sex life is often on the wane or nonexistent. A man cannot force a woman to be sexual when she does not want to be. Being persistent about being sexual just drives a deeper wedge in the relationship. It typically takes couples a long time to recover their sexual relationship. If the couple can significantly reduce negativity and enhance their emotional intimacy, their sexual relationship can often be revived. However, the emotional reparation of a marriage takes time. Therefore, the husband needs to move the focus off of sex onto what changes he needs to make in order to reconnect with his wife. If a man needs to masturbate to relieve his sexual pressure, so be it. He should never threaten to have his sexual needs met by someone outside the relationship. This statement would blame the wife for not performing and undermine the integrity of the relationship.

If the husband typically pursues the wife sexually, and the wife is refusing because of their marital difficulties, then the husband needs to stop making requests. He is probably driving his wife further away emotionally. The goal is to improve the relationship so that the wife will want to pursue a sexual relationship with her husband. The husband will need to wait patiently for his wife to pursue him. This can be extremely difficult for men. However, if the man doesn't change his approach, the likelihood of sex over time becomes even less likely.

In order for a woman to pursue sex, a relationship sometimes needs to be relatively healthy for a period of time. A man's patience is of the utmost importance. When a man is impatient about the lack of sex, it slows down the process. The man needs to keep in mind that the short-term goal of having sex should not override the long-term goal of having a happy marriage with a healthy sex life.

The majority of relationship struggles occur when a husband is not meeting the emotional needs of his wife. When this occurs for a period of time, the sexual life of a couple will be affected, and men are often not aware that this is even occurring. Therefore, the emphasis for men needs to be on meeting the emotional needs of their wives. This is where the focus needs to be: not on achieving an orgasm, but on emotional closeness. When a wife is feeling emotionally close with her husband, she is more likely to want to be with him sexually. Men need to focus on listening to their wives, being attentive to their wives, not criticizing or blaming their wives, etc. This is how husbands can revive their sexual lives.

The sexual issues discussed so far have to do with the differences in sexual desire. These differences have to be worked out in healthy relationships, and they are exacerbated during marital difficulties. Occasionally, sexual problems in a relationship can have a physiological component, in addition to an emotional component. Problems such as impotency, premature ejaculation, and vaginitis may need to be addressed with a medical workup. Emotional issues may intensify these problems, but they also need to be looked at on a physiological level. Work with a sex therapist may be appropriate for these sexual issues.

Of course, in some relationships, women have a stronger sexual desire than men, and men can be the ones to sexually withdraw. The focus is less on which gender is doing the sexual pursuing and distancing. The issue is becoming more aware of these relationship dynamics.

Frequently it can take time for a sexual relationship to be revived. What we really want is to revive the marriage. A healthy sexual relationship mirrors a healthy marriage.

Key Points

- A couple's budget needs to reflect their values.

- Chores need to feel equitable.

- When parenting, the disciplinarian and the emotional caretaker need to coordinate their approaches.

- The *Whispering Technique* can be a very effective parenting approach.

- A couple typically needs a strong emotional connection in order to have a healthy sexual relationship.

5

The Vision

In order to move in a positive direction, one needs to know where one is going. A couple needs to create an image in their minds of what their relationship is going to look like. For example, they can imagine their relationship with a certain degree of harmony. They can imagine that if a challenging issue comes up in their relationship, they can address it with each other respectfully and with a certain degree of grace.

If couples go back and remember when they were courting each other, the memory can tap back into the initial attraction and appeal. They can remember how they would go out of the way for one another. At that time, they would do almost anything for their partner. They felt in love. They enjoyed their conversations with each other. They enjoyed time with each other, even in silence. They enjoyed doing things with each other. They would look forward to the next time they would see each other. All of these qualities just don't vanish. However, they can gradually diminish when conflict and strife enter the relationship. Couples can forget what brought them together in the first place.

The importance of vision is not to lose this perspective. The person that you married—the essence of that person—is still there. One may treat each other in a mean, nasty, or disconnected way, but the core qualities of the person that you married still exist. The challenge is to rediscover these qualities. Once a couple returns to treating each other with respect, these qualities can begin to reemerge.

Early in the relationship, couples almost always treat each other with respect. The attraction and appeal they feel discourages disrespectful behavior. However, time gradually erodes the intensity of the attraction and appeal. How does one not lose sight of the partner that they married?

That deep feeling of love may diminish when interactions become ugly, but the love doesn't vanish. It is typically lying dormant.

It is important for couples not to lose sight of this. Without a vision of what once was and where a couple can return, the couple swirls in their interactions of strife. The couple needs to create a joint image of getting along well, of enjoying each other's company, of enjoying conversations about each other's worlds, of enjoying events or silent moments together.

Occasionally I will tell my clients the following: "Just imagine that you can deeply enjoy being with your spouse again. See this image in your mind, feel it; you can create it. You need to reexperience those qualities to regain them. This will give you the sense of hope of what's possible. This will give you the motivation to do the hard work. This will give you the hope that you can recapture what you once had, but in a fuller, more mature relationship." To create a vibrant, pleasurable relationship, a couple needs to create this image in their minds and then do the hard work that will take them there. Love can be recaptured.

THE HIGHER ROAD

Dave and Theresa came to me on the brink of divorce. In fact, Dave initially came to me by himself, upset that his wife of seventeen years wanted to divorce him. He was emotionally distraught, since he loved his wife and his two teenage children. Dave wanted to know what he could do to stop the divorce process. His wife was very strong-willed. Once she made up her mind, she was very unlikely to change it.

I asked Dave he if he could get his wife to attend one of our sessions. Since his wife felt that she was not the problem and Dave was, we framed this meeting as a chance for Theresa to tell me what Dave's problems were. Even if Theresa refused to attend couples treatment, with her feedback, I could address the issues that Dave needed to work on anyway.

During this meeting, Theresa told me how emotionally withdrawn Dave was. Dave never came home from work when he said he would, and Dave spent an inordinate amount of time golfing on the weekends.

Theresa had become fed up with Dave's golfing. He would golf most of the weekend, and would drink with the guys after golf.

Theresa felt that she and the kids were being neglected. Theresa felt like a golf widow, and her perception was that the kids didn't have a relationship with their father. Theresa operated as a single parent, rarely consulting with Dave about parenting issues. She figured if she was a "single parent" anyway, she would move out with the kids. At this point she was actively looking for another place to live closer to work. She wanted to do this by the summer so the kids could adjust before the new school year. With a clear plan in place, Dave would have to change quickly to avert it.

Overall, Theresa did not feel emotionally connected to Dave and disapproved of how underinvolved he was in the kids' lives. During our meeting, Dave expressed how much he loved and cared for Theresa. Theresa seemed miffed, saying, "If you loved me and the kids the way you say you do, why are you not a part of our lives?" Dave said he didn't realize how strong Theresa's feelings were. Theresa insisted that she had communicated this for years.

Theresa brought up an incident in which she was gravely ill, to the point of not knowing whether she would live or not. On a particular frightening day, Theresa asked Dave to come to the hospital. Dave refused since he had an "essential" business meeting. This incident represented for Theresa how unavailable Dave was. Even in her most frightening moment, he could not be there for her.

When Dave heard this story, he defended his decision making, which further angered Theresa. I coached Dave to respond differently. His habitually defensive response to this story infuriated Theresa. Initially she would attack Dave. She would eventually emotionally withdraw from Dave when she did not feel heard.

Dave was able to acknowledge that he felt bad about his decision not to go to the hospital. He had underestimated how sick Theresa was and put too much importance on this business meeting. He said that his family should always come before business, and he regretted his decision. Finally, Theresa felt heard.

Dave's work was to become more emotionally intelligent. Dave had high cognitive intelligence, as reflected in his professional degree and successful business. However, his emotional intelligence was on the lower end of the continuum. Emotional intelligence refers to awareness of oneself and one's feelings, emotional restraint, awareness of another person's feelings, and relationship management (Goleman 2005). Dave certainly needed to become more aware of his feelings for Theresa. He needed to restrain his defensive reaction to her, to be more open to her feelings, and to do a better job of managing his relationship with her. Although cognitive intelligence is relatively stable, emotional intelligence can be learned.

When talking about the hospital incident, I coached Dave to be open to Theresa's hurt rather than be defensive. Although Theresa had shared her hurt with Dave about the hospital incident many times, this was the first time she felt heard. Dave expressed remorse about not being there for her when Theresa really needed him. Dave expressed his determination to emotionally support Theresa from this point forward. Based on history, Theresa doubted that Dave was capable of doing this. However, Dave seemed determined to prove that he was capable of emotionally supporting her.

Theresa had a very critical communication style. She could be very direct and did not mince her words. Sometimes her delivery could be cutting. Since she was so upset at Dave's emotional withdrawal over the years, she was not willing to look at her own delivery. She felt so angry that either Dave needed to change, or "I am definitely out of this marriage." Her line in the sand was pretty clear. Since Dave was determined to make his marriage work, he was willing to do whatever it took to save the marriage, even if Theresa was not willing to look at herself.

The first stage of work was for Dave to make substantial changes in his relationship so that Theresa did not want to move out. Then the goal was to sustain these changes. Once Theresa felt more hopeful about the marriage, the focus could shift to her. As long as her comments were critical, they created an emotional distance in their relationship. Theresa would eventually need to learn to communicate her hurt and anger directly without criticizing her husband.

In divorce prevention work, Dave kept a journal of his statements to Theresa and recorded Theresa's response. This kept Dave vigilant about how he was communicating with Theresa and what her response was. In day-to-day life, a spouse always gives feedback about how successful their partner's delivery is. The skill is to tune in to this feedback. Dave would first report his successes to me and then would review his less successful statements.

Theresa would also keep a journal. We would first review Dave's successful comments that he may not have recognized. It is very important to reinforce when someone is communicating successfully. Then we would review the unsuccessful comments that Dave may not have recognized.

The goal was to increase Dave's emotional intelligence in the context of his relationship with Theresa. The purpose was to become more aware of how he communicated with Theresa and to become aware of the impact of his statements on her. Theresa's responses gave Dave feedback on how skillfully he was communicating.

One of Dave's communication patterns was to defend himself, and he was not even conscious of this process. As Theresa was typically critical, it was natural for Dave to defend himself. However, since Theresa was not ready to become noncritical, Dave needed to elevate himself above the criticism. He needed to be able to filter out the criticism and be responsive to the underlying issue that Theresa was communicating. When he could not identify being defensive, my role was to point this out. I would also teach him how to filter out the criticism in Theresa's message so that he could be open and responsive to the underlying issue.

For the first time in seventeen years, Theresa felt that she was finally being heard. Although her communication was still critical, she had fewer issues about which to be critical since Dave was finally listening to her. Typically, if someone is critical, it is difficult to filter through the criticism to hear what the person's complaints are. However, Dave was so determined to save his marriage that he worked very diligently at being able to filter through Theresa's critical statements and hear her concerns.

Theresa never did move out. Dave was able to make enough changes that Theresa decided not to separate. Although she was not confident that

Dave's changes would be sustained over the long run, Dave was determined to stay consistent with the changes he was making in his communication style. Dave found other ways to be attentive to his wife, including touching her more affectionately and planning weekends away.

Dave also became aware that golf was his way of dealing with the emotional distance in his marriage. Since he was not getting his emotional needs met at home, he withdrew into his golf game. Dave is now playing golf once a week and at a time that is less disruptive to the family. He is now getting more enjoyment from his family than he ever got from his golf game.

So how does a couple recapture their love? It's done through hard work. Who is going to do this hard work? It starts with the individual. If we think our spouse is going to change, it probably isn't going to happen. When we realize that we individually have the power to transform a relationship, we can make it happen. However, it means taking the high road. Dave is a good example of someone who took the high road.

Taking the high road is being very diligent about how you speak to your spouse and making sure your initial statements are devoid of criticism and blame. Taking the high road means when your spouse criticizes you, blames you, or tells you what to do, you are able to filter out his or her inappropriate comment and respond to the essence of the statement. The more difficult challenge comes when your spouse criticizes or blames you. The natural tendency is to return the criticism or blame in return. The high road means not doing that. Holding a vision of the relationship can help one respond the right way.

When a person is criticized or blamed by their spouse, it can be challenging not to respond in kind. It is important not to react impulsively. If your spouse is upset about something, taking a more inquisitive approach could help you understand what's bothering them. If you love this person, you don't want them to feel upset. If you did something to upset them, you want to see if you can remedy the situation. If your spouse needs to express their upset, it's important to support them whether or not you were the source of it. If you are the reason they are upset, you ultimately don't want to be. If you are listening, you may be able to learn what you could do differently that would be healing for the relationship. This kind of response would demonstrate a high degree of emotional maturity. Although it is very challenging to do, one can make tremendous strides towards the vision being created.

CONCESSION AND COMPROMISE

How do couples resolve conflict? It happens through concession and compromise. When one is single, one doesn't have to report to anyone. One can do as they please and not have to worry about the implications on someone else.

However, when one is married, he or she must take into account another person's feelings. A person who is married needs to be aware of the implications of his or her behavior on the spouse.

If one is single, what time one comes home from work or how one spends money doesn't impact anyone else. When one is married, lack of punctuality and excessive spending can be problematic.

A person sometimes needs to compromise wishes and desires in order to be successful in a marriage. The focus is no longer exclusively on the individual, but on the relationship. One also needs to inquire what his or her spouse's wishes and desires are. After talking together, a couple makes concessions and compromises. A plan can then emerge which is respectful to both. Sometimes the plan will meet both spouses' needs to some degree (compromise) and sometimes the plan will predominantly meet one person's needs (concession) depending on who feels more strongly about the issue.

Parents constantly concede and compromise their needs in order to be responsive to their children. We need to do the same with our spouses in order to achieve our vision of marital harmony.

RELATIONSHIP UNDER REPAIR

Steve and Rachel were having work done to their house. When Steve arrived home from work one night, he said to Rachel, "Who moved the vacuum?" Rachel responded by saying, "Don't blame me!" Steve said back, "I'm not blaming you. There were workmen in the house today, so I'm wondering where they moved the vacuum."

This is a nice example of repairing a potential conflict. Steve's initial statement, "Who moved the vacuum?" could easily have been interpreted as an accusatory statement. Rachel perceived that Steve thought she moved the vacuum as opposed to a worker having done so.

Steve was irritated that the vacuum was not in the closet where it typically was, and his statement revealed his annoyance. When Rachel responded to his statement defensively, he picked up on it and corrected his intention: "I didn't mean to accuse you, I was just wondering where the vacuum was."

Steve's initial question could have been, "Rachel, do you know where the vacuum is?" In the right tone of voice, this would be a question of curiosity that would be unlikely to elicit defensiveness. However, if Steve said, "Where the hell is the vacuum?" conflict would likely ensue.

Steve was perceptive enough to recognize that Rachel's reaction was defensive. He absorbed this feedback and was nimble enough to clarify his statement. In other words, he self-corrected. If he had said, "Why are you getting so defensive?" the interaction would probably have escalated. When he self-corrected, Rachel's next statement was not defensive or attacking. This was Steve's feedback that his statement was successful.

A couple's relationship begins to deteriorate when a couple is unable to repair their relationship conflict. Half of marriages end in divorce, and another percentage of marriages are either loveless marriages or marriages of convenience. Clearly, the majority of marriages are unable to repair their own conflict. In order to avoid becoming another statistic, a couple needs professional intervention at the point at which they are unable to repair their own relationship conflict.

The goal of the work is for couples to be able to repair their relationships. Initially, many couples are not aware of their relationship dynamics. The purpose of this book is to help couples become more aware of their interactions so that they can repair their own conflict. However, a couple in significant distress may need professional intervention. When couples are in conflict, sometimes they are so immersed in the conflict that they cannot see it clearly. A major purpose of the professional is to make individuals conscious of their relationship dynamics. Once people are aware of these relationship dynamics, they can begin to change their own behaviors.

I CAN TALK TO YOU ABOUT ANYTHING

The ultimate goal of professional intervention is to help one talk with his or her spouse about anything. Initially in professional work, couples talk about the "hotter" issues—the most difficult issues. These are the issues that couples would be extremely unlikely to resolve on their own. Couples typically use communication patterns that are ineffective for resolving these differences. When couples are unsuccessful, the professional can guide the couple to navigate successfully.

The professional will have the couple talk about the issue. Typically early in divorce prevention treatment, the couple will take turns talking to the professional about the issue. The professional does not allow the couple to interrupt one another. The problematic communication pattern already begins to change because unlike at home, the spouse is more likely to listen to what their partner is saying within this structured plan. Since spouses are initially communicating through the professional, the affect is significantly moderated. This structure keeps the dialogue from escalating and allows the couple to hear what the partner's concerns are. The role of the professional is to help clarify the issues.

As the couple advances in treatment, they will eventually be able to talk directly with each other about the issues. Early in treatment this is difficult since the couple tends to repeat the unsuccessful interactions that they have already attempted at home. When the couple talks directly to each other during the meeting, there are important guidelines for the couple to observe. These are referred to as the Rules for Healthy Dialogue, which are also listed in the Appendix.

1. *No interrupting.* It is important that a spouse is able to talk about his or her concerns and issues without interruption. This rule also significantly increases the likelihood that the other spouse is listening. If the couple interrupts one another, the dialogue tends to escalate rather quickly.

2. *No criticism.* If a spouse if criticized, he or she will likely respond with a defensive or critical statement. All critical statements can be transformed into noncritical statements. The skill of the professional is to teach couples how to do this. The professional can also point out the more subtle critical statements, such as rhetorical questions.

3. *No blame.* Many spouses tend to blame one another. Since change only occurs within the individual, the focus needs to be on what changes an individual is willing to make.

4. *Not being parental.* It is disrespectful to talk to your spouse as if you are talking to a child. Parental statements can always be transformed.

5. *Not being analytical.* It is also disrespectful to analyze why your spouse behaves the way that he or she does, for example, by saying "You are angry because your father was so mean to you." This makes an individual a psychoanalyst instead of a spouse. Only an individual has the right to self-analyze.

6. *No kitchen sinking.* The term kitchen sinking refers to throwing everything in, including the kitchen sink. It is important for couples to talk about one issue at a time. Once a couple resolves an issue, they can move on to the next. Dealing with multiple issues at the same time typically escalates conflict.

7. *One can only express a perspective twice.* An individual is free to share his or her perspective or memory of a situation. If the spouse disagrees with that perspective or memory, the individual has one more oppor-

tunity to express his or her perspective or memory. If the other spouse continues to have a different perspective or memory, the couple should then halt that particular dialogue, and basically agree to disagree.

8. *Discuss issues before problem solving.* It is important to discuss an issue before attempting to problem solve. A couple needs to brainstorm the underlying parameters of an issue before attempting to resolve it. Men have a greater tendency to prematurely problem solve.

9. *Focus on positives.* It is important to comment when a spouse is doing something well. For example, if a spouse is having decent conversations with the kids, it is more effective to comment on this rather than how you hated when your spouse used to yell at the kids. Commenting on positives can help increase the frequency of positive events. Everyone appreciates praise.

10. *Explain versus defend.* When couples have a history of attacking and defending themselves, sometimes an individual can continue to defend himself or herself, even when he or she is not being attacked in that moment. For example, if an individual comes home late from work, they should explain what happened rather than defend being late. When a person defends himself or herself, it increases the likelihood that their spouse will attack him or her.

11. *Stop after three attacking statements.* During couples work, the professional will typically intervene after each attacking statement, so this rule applies more to couples talking about issues in between meetings. If one spouse perceives that three attacking statements have occurred, then the couple needs to agree to halt the conversation. They can agree to return to the conversation in a less heated moment, or they bring the issue back to the next meeting with the professional.

When couples talk directly to each other in a meeting with the professional, the role of the professional is to make sure that couples are observing these *Rules for Healthy Dialogue.* When an individual makes an "inappropriate" statement, it is essential that the professional have this person "redo" the statement. If the individual is unable to redo the statement, the professional can role model how to do this. This is how the professional becomes a teacher. The professional is teaching the spouse how to communicate well. Later in the work, the spouse may be able to self-correct himself or herself.

If the couple is talking about a recent or past conflict, the task is to not rehash who said what to whom. Couples often have different perceptions of how a conflict transpired. It could be helpful for the professional to hear each spouse's perception of a marital conflict. However, it is not important for the professional to reach consensus on reconstructing the conflict. Inevitably the spouses are going to perceive and remember the conflict differently. What is important is that the difference between the couple is resolved. The couple may talk about the unresolved issue in the presence of the professional, so the professional can intervene when the dialogue goes off track.

During direct dialogue with a spouse, if an individual is aware that his or her comment will not stay within the *Rules for Healthy Dialogue*, that person can have a "sidebar" with the professional. Although the spouse can hear this conversation, the professional works with the individual to make sure that his or her statement stays within the *Rules for Healthy Dialogue*. The other spouse is not allowed to comment on the sidebar. Once the individual is able to make an appropriate statement, he or she will make this statement directly to his or her spouse.

Remember that any attacking statement can be rephrased. This is essential in order for a couple to communicate successfully. Attacking statements routinely get a defensive and/or attacking response in return. A defensive or attacking response can often be feedback that the initial statement was attacking. So if your spouse responds in a defensive or attacking manner, always examine closely whether your statement attacked your spouse in anyway.

If the professional can get a couple to communicate within the *Rules for Healthy Dialogue*, the likelihood of a successful dialogue increases significantly. The communication between the couple becomes clear. With clear communication, the recipient can become more skilled at understanding the essence of what their spouse is trying to communicate. There may be underlying relationship themes, but the underlying issues will be much more apparent when the dialogue doesn't get muddled by poor communication skills. When the communication is clear, it is typically sufficient for having couples resolve their differences.

In this work, focusing on the couple's past isn't essential. Relationship issues from the past almost always manifest themselves in the present. If a person has been verbally abusive in the past, it is likely that he or she will continue to be verbally abusive. Also, most couples prefer to address current issues since they directly impact the relationship. Once a couple resolves most of the present day issues, they can consider examining issues from earlier in their relationship. The focus is less on resolving these past issues than on communicating how these past issues were hurtful. This can help create healing in the relationship.

The work also does not need to focus on family-of-origin issues. Understanding how your parents treated you as a child or how your parents treated each other in your childhood may be interesting, but awareness of these dynamics doesn't necessarily change how you treat your spouse or children. For example, if one of your parents was critical during your childhood, the likelihood of you being critical as an adult is pretty good. The relevant issue is becoming aware of how you are critical in the present and working diligently on being noncritical. If one can do this in the present, one can transform the influence of the past.

Initially in the work, the professional may ask couples not to talk to each other about the hot issues outside of the meetings. The reason for this is that couples have already attempted to do this on their own but have been unsuccessful. They need a professional to facilitate those conversations. In addition, couples tend to talk about the most difficult issues first.

The reason for working with a professional is to create a safe environment in which the couple can talk about issues. The professional should not allow a couple's communication to escalate out of control. The *Rules for Healthy Dialogue* help to prevent this. The professional wants to create an environment in which spouses feel comfortable fully expressing themselves without hurting one another. It is important for each spouse to be heard.

As a couple moves from talking about the most difficult issues to the more moderate issues, the couple can eventually begin to practice the skills they are learning outside the session. However, if a couple begins to escalate as they are talking about an issue, the couple needs to stop immediately and bring the issue to the next meeting.

When the couple addresses most of their issues, then the couple is ready to cut back on the frequency of meetings. However, it is still important for the couple to be followed so that they do not relapse. One doesn't want the couple's relationship to deteriorate due to ending counseling prematurely. It is important for the couple to interact successfully on their own for a good period of time before they end this professional work.

If a couple is able to employ some of the strategies that a professional uses, it will increase the likelihood of success. If a couple can learn to eliminate negativity, they can address the issues that are blocking their emotional connection. If a couple can learn to talk with each other in a respectful, dignified manner over a sustained period of time, they can recapture the love that brought them together. Couples *can* learn the skills to save their marriage and prevent divorce.

Ellen and Don was one such couple. They came to me while Ellen was having an affair with Robert. Ellen was very clear in our first meeting that she did not intend to give up this affair. However, she was not ready to divorce her husband of twenty-two years. I interpreted Ellen's contradictions as not wanting to give up her relationship with Robert until she was convinced that her marriage could be saved.

Counseling began with the couple talking about their relationship with each other. They talked about how they were initially attracted to each other in college. They took me through the trials and tribulations of their relationship. They said they had a child soon after marrying and talked about how they had grown distant over the years. Ellen had a self-proclaimed "bossy style," and Don was emotionally distant. Ellen had a decent group of friends and enjoyed socializing with them. Don tended to be more of a homebody, enjoying his after dinner martinis, TV shows and books. They had grown distant over the years, but caring for their teenage daughter had kept them together.

When Ellen met Robert, she was not looking for an affair. She found someone who was interested in her and someone with whom she emotionally connected. Don eventually found out about the affair and sought out professional help.

What Ellen and Don mostly needed to do was emotionally reconnect with each other. They talked about their dissatisfactions. They talked about how they had grown distant over the years. It became clear that they still had loving feelings for one another. My primary role was to point out if Ellen became bossy or draw Don back into the conversation if he emotionally withdrew.

In our fourth meeting, Ellen declared that she had ended the relationship with Robert. Our initial meetings clarified for Ellen that she still had feelings for Don. She now wanted to fully focus her attention on saving her marriage and did not want Robert to be a distraction.

Over the months Ellen and Don continued to talk with each other about their marriage and rediscovered ways to connect with each other. They both enjoyed travel, and every fall they would go to Europe together, traveling the fields and peaks of France, Spain, and Italy. They would relay their wondrous moments with each other. They would return from these trips relishing the discovery of remote villages in the Pyrenees Mountains of Spain. They also enjoyed the process of redoing their aging kitchen together, even enjoying the gentle banter of deciding what knobs to put on their cabinets.

This was a couple that really rediscovered each other, recapturing some of the magic that initially brought them together. Ellen and Don had reached a place in their marriage where they had never been before. Their marriage had the deep connection of a mature relationship. The comfort and mutual fondness between them was palpable.

With the right approach, maybe your marriage could also be saved.

Key Points

- It is important to create a vision of how you want your relationship to be.

- Each individual is encouraged to take the higher road.

- It is vital for a couple to concede, compromise, and repair conflict.

- Following the *Rules for Healthy Dialogue* is an excellent way to minimize relationship conflict.

Appendix

Rules for Healthy Dialogue

1. No interrupting.

2. No criticism.

3. No blame.

4. Not being parental.

5. Not being analytical.

6. No kitchen sinking.

7. One can only express a perspective twice.

8. Discuss issues before problem solving.

9. Focus on positives.

10. Explain versus defend.

11. Stop after three attacking statements.

References

Goleman, Daniel P. *Emotional Intelligence.* New York: Bantam Books, 2005.

Gottman, John M. and Nan Silver. *Seven Principles for Making Marriage Work: A Practical Guide from the Country's Foremost Relationship Expert.* CA: Three Rivers Press, 2000.

Gray, John. *Men Are from Mars, Women Are from Venus: A Practical Guide for Improving Communication and Getting What You Want in Your Relationships.* New York: Harper Collins Publishers, 1992.

978-0-595-38604-8
0-595-38604-0

LaVergne, TN USA
15 October 2009
161027LV00011B/149/A